EMMAUS

the way of faith

STAGE 3: GROWTH

EMMAUS
the way of faith

STAGE 3: GROWTH

Christian Lifestyle

Four short modules for growing Christians

Stephen Cottrell, Steven Croft,

John Finney, Felicity Lawson and Robert Warren

Second edition

 CHURCH HOUSE
PUBLISHING

Church House Publishing
Church House
Great Smith Street
London SW1P 3NZ

ISBN 0 7151 4006 X

Second edition published 2003
by Church House Publishing.

First edition published 1996 by
The National Society/Church House Publishing
and The Bible Society.

Tel: 020 7898 1594;
Fax: 020 7898 1449;
Email: copyright@c-of-e.org.uk.

CD-ROM created by Ambit New Media
www.ambitnewmedia.com

Cover design by Church House Publishing
Cover photograph copyright © Getty Images

Printed in England by Biddles Ltd,
Guildford and King's Lynn

Contents

Part 4   Called into life

CD-ROM contents

- *members' handouts and supplementary handouts as PDF files;*

- Emmaus *posters;*

- *twelve handouts used for introducing the idea of* Emmaus *to churches;*

- *three PowerPoint presentations (which can also be adapted into OHP slides) for introducing the idea of* Emmaus *to churches;*

- Emmaus *Resources Catalogue;*

- *Links to the* Emmaus *web site;*

- *Help page.*

Acknowledgements

The authors and publisher gratefully acknowledge permission to reproduce copyright material in this book. Every effort has been made to trace and contact copyright holders. If there are any inadvertent omissions, we apologize to those concerned and undertake to include suitable acknowledgements in all future editions.

The Scripture quotations contained herein are form *The New Revised Standard Version of the Bible*, copyright © 1989 by the Division of Christian Education of the National Council of the Churches of Christ in the USA and are used by permission. All rights reserved.

Extracts from *Common Worship: Services and Prayers for the Church of England* (Church House Publishing, 2000) are copyright © The Archbishops' Council 2000 and are reproduced by permission.

Extracts from T. S. Eliot, Choruses from 'The Rock', *Collected Poems 1909-1962*, Faber and Faber Ltd. Reproduced by permission of the publishers.

Extracts from Luke T. Johnson, *Sharing Possessions*, SCM Press, 1986. Reproduced by permission of the publisher.

Extracts from Leanne Payne, *The Healing Presence*, copyright © Leanne Payne 1989. Used by permission of Kingsway Communications, Lottbridge Drove, Eastbourne.

Extracts from Tom Smail, *The Forgotten Father*, Hodder & Stoughton, 1980. Used by permission of the publisher.

Introducing the *Emmaus* Growth materials

What are the Growth materials?

The *Emmaus* Growth courses are published in four books (see diagram below). Each book contains four or five short modules on aspects of Christian living.

Each module contains up to five individual sessions (more in *Your Kingdom Come*).

What is the purpose of the Growth materials?

The *Emmaus* Growth materials are intended to offer Christians an opportunity to deepen their understanding of Christian living and discipleship. They may be used as a follow-on from a nurture course – whether you've already used *Emmaus* or not.

The materials may be used with new Christians, to enable them to lay firm foundations, and to help more mature Christians take a fresh look at familiar topics.

What's in each of the Growth books?

Knowing God	Growing as a Christian
Christian Lifestyle	Your Kingdom Come

Knowing God

4 Modules

Knowing God	Growing as a Christian
Christian Lifestyle	Your Kingdom Come

1   Living the Gospel (4 sessions)

A simple course on sharing our faith with others who make up our own network of relationships.

2   Knowing the Father (4 sessions)

Our experience of God leading to an appreciation of God as Holy Trinity.

3   Knowing Jesus (4 sessions)

The person of Jesus and a relationship with him as Lord.

4   Come, Holy Spirit (4 sessions)

The work of the Holy Spirit in the life of individual Christians, in the Church and in the world.

Growing as a Christian

5 Modules

Knowing God	Growing as a Christian
Christian Lifestyle	Your Kingdom Come

I   Growing in prayer (4 sessions)

Different methods and understandings of prayer, including practical help and encouragement. The course is based around the Lord's Prayer.

2   Growing in the Scriptures (5 sessions)

The nature and meaning of the Scriptures and practical help in understanding and reading the Bible.

3   Being church (4 sessions)

What does it mean to belong? Different models and understandings of the Church.

4   Growing in worship — understanding the sacraments (5 sessions)

An exploration of Christian worship as an unfolding celebration of the Easter mystery and of the sacraments as communion with the risen Lord.

5   Life, death and Christian hope (3 sessions)

An exploration of the Christian hope, the last things and the Christian attitude to death.

Christian Lifestyle

4 Modules

Knowing God	Growing as a Christian
Christian Lifestyle	Your Kingdom Come

I   Living images (4 sessions)

There is a search for meaning in life in today's society and a longing to live life to the full. But what does it mean to do that? How can we be fully human?

2   Overcoming evil (5 sessions)

As soon as we seek to be fully human we discover problems. People are not perfect and life is not fair. There is a flaw in the whole of creation. The reality, which the Christian tradition calls sin, is understood as being like gravity. How do we understand and address this aspect of life?

3   Personal identity (5 sessions)

How do we understand ourselves so we can love others? This session explores how that true self can be rightly affirmed, nourished and expressed in life.

4   Called into life (4 sessions)

This course is intended to help every baptized believer to know more about what it means to have a vocation – not just for the work we do, if we are employed, but for who we are and how we live the whole of our lives before God.

Your Kingdom Come

2 Modules

Knowing God	Growing as a Christian
Christian Lifestyle	Your Kingdom Come

I   The Beatitudes: Your kingdom come among us
(6 sessions)

An explanation of the Beatitudes and an examination of the values by which Christians are called to live and shape their lifestyles. Such values call us to 'live the kingdom – now'. It is a costly calling to live life differently from the culture in which we are set.

2   The kingdom: Your kingdom come through us (10 sessions)

An exploration of the kingdom and a look at the actions Christians are called to take in seeking to be part of God's compassionate concern to bring all human experience, and all creation, to their fulfilment in and through Christ. The kingdom is explored by considering three Old Testament themes on which Jesus' teaching about the kingdom is founded: Sabbath, Jubilee and Shalom.

How do I use the Growth materials?

Each Growth book has four or five modules (two for *Your Kingdom Come*). Within each module there are four or five sessions.

Of course, you can be as flexible as you wish with the material. You do not need to use each of the sessions and you can cover the material in whatever order and over whatever period of time suits the needs of your group.

You may choose to use some of the sessions or modules with an enquirers' group. Some groups have found the 'Personal identity' module from *Christian Lifestyle* particularly appropriate.

Leading a growth course

The materials have been designed so that courses can be led by lay people or clergy, but in most churches lay-led groups will be better. Experience does help, but the material here has been used successfully by people who have never led groups before.

There is some teaching input to be delivered in each session, but this comes in manageable chunks with detailed and straightforward notes. The main emphasis is not on the leader talking to the group, but on facilitating sharing, reflection, Bible study and discussion.

Your group may already have explored the basics of Christian faith in the *Emmaus* Nurture course or in some other way. Or you may be an established house group looking for a new direction. Or perhaps you are a group of Christians coming together for the first time in your church to go deeper in faith.

Whichever kind of group you will be leading, the leader's main task in all these courses will be to encourage and enable exploration and discussion. Growth in the Christian life is not just about accumulating knowledge. There are things to learn, but growth is about initiation into a way of life, rather than just gaining possession of a body of information.

In engaging with this material, group members will be encouraged to think deeply about their own experience of life and so enter into dialogue with the Christian tradition. In this way people will make the tradition their own. Faith will not be second-hand knowledge, but first-hand experience. This understanding is central to everything that happens on the Way of Faith.

No two groups are the same, so it is important for each group leader to feel free to adapt the material to suit the particular needs and gifts of individuals within each particular group. Don't feel you need to tackle all the courses in one book, or do them in the order given. Take them one at a time. Then, towards the end of each course, if your group is staying together, think and pray and talk together about whether to tackle another – or use some different material.

Preparation

A separate booklet, *Leading an Emmaus Group*, contains helpful advice on leading and running any kind of nurture or growth group.

In your preparation for each course and for each meeting of the group you will need to bear the following things in mind:

1   Running the meeting

Aim
Each of the Growth modules has three, four or five sessions. At the beginning of the course the aim is clearly stated. Before you do anything else make sure that you are clear about the aim of the module and the aim of each session.

Content
Make sure you are familiar with the content of each session. Try to be reasonably familiar with all the material, especially the teaching input, so that you can lead the meeting without endlessly referring to the notes, and without your head being stuck in a book. But of course you will need these leaders' notes with you. That is what they are for!

Each group member also has a handout sheet for each session. This contains material that forms the basis of the group's work in this session. This book contains the leaders' notes plus photocopiable masters for a double-sided A4-handout for group members (these may also be downloaded from the CD-ROM). These usually need to be given out at the beginning of each meeting.

For some sessions, additional handouts are available, if you wish to use them. This is all clearly explained in the leaders' notes.

Method
We aim to use a variety of teaching methods. All the sessions in the growth courses call for different ways of engaging with the material – teaching input from the leader, one-to-one discussion, splitting the group into smaller units, presentations to one another and, in some courses, art and craft work. Do not shy away from using the more creative and experiential parts of the material. Despite initial embarrassment, many people will find these parts the most enjoyable and stimulating.

People learn in different ways. For some this will be through listening to the teaching input and reading what is on the handouts. For others it will be by appropriating the teaching input – reflecting it back in group discussions and making it their own. For others it will be by articulating their own insights, knowledge and experiences. For most of us it will be a combination of all these. Certainly, what people remember most from any group is what they say themselves. If for no other reason than this, we need to encourage discussion.

The courses aim at a creative dialogue between the tradition of the Church and our own experience of life. This is the way we will grow into mature Christians who are able to live a Christian life in and for the world.

Leading the group

Two key words can help in effective leading of *Emmaus* groups, especially in this part of the course: conducting and empowering.

It is all too easy for the leader to feel too responsible and so end up doing everything. It is much better to see the leader's role as like that of the conductor of an orchestra. While working to a prepared script, members of a good orchestra put themselves, and thereby their own interpretation, into the music. For this to happen, each person needs to play to the best of their ability and to harmonize their contribution to the whole. Sometimes this is done by keeping silent. The task of the conductor is to draw out each contribution and to harmonize them, building something unique in the life of the group as a whole. This can be done by recognizing those who have gifts of hospitality, meditation, friendship, practical action, ability to create visual aids, teaching, etc. and allowing them to make their contribution. Equally, in discussion different people will emerge with different contributions – some will see the connection with the Old Testament, others will only be interested in how it connects with life, someone else may have read widely and see connections in other ways. The good leader knows the instruments each person plays, and draws them out to enrich the whole. At any one session the good leader may not do any evident 'leading' – just as the conductor of an orchestra is the one person who does not play a musical instrument.

Empowering is the principle of helping people to believe in themselves, their value to God and to the group, and the worth of what they have to contribute. The task of the leader is not that of traditional teacher ('let me tell you the answer'), but that of helping others to make their own discoveries and to make the truth their own ('now I see', 'now I can . . .'). A good leader will help a group to break out of dependency into a creative group who take responsibility and initiatives of their own – individually and together. It is important to watch for this, and to affirm all such steps whenever they emerge.

2 The people who make up the group

Any group consists of individuals, all with different needs and cares, all loved by God, and all at different points on the journey.

If your group is a new one and is coming together for the first time, you will need to take especial care over the first few meetings so that everyone gets to know everyone else and can share part of their own story. In the early meetings, building community is at least as important as covering the material. The introductory exercises in each of the sessions will be important here.

As the sessions continue and strangers begin to become friends, try to make sure everyone remains involved. This does not necessarily mean ensuring that everyone speaks, but it does mean that everyone is engaged. When planning the meetings ask yourself: Is there opportunity to speak, especially to ask a question? Is everyone able to make a contribution if they want to? You may need to try to contain people who are saying too much. Splitting the group up, or deliberately asking someone else's view, are two ways of handling this.

Difficult questions

One of the greatest fears for those leading a course like this is fear of the difficult question. Some leaders deal with this by making it very hard for anyone to say anything. This is not the aim of *Emmaus*. The Growth courses are concerned to teach people the faith, but this is best done by encouraging questions and sharing experiences. If you do not know the answer to a question, say so. (However, you may also offer to come back with a response at the next session, which will allow you time to give the question some thought or ask the advice of others.)

Ask the rest of the group for suggestions. You are not expected to be the expert. You are expected to help others voice their questions and anxieties as they grow in faith.

For some questions, there may not be an answer. For many questions, help can be available elsewhere in your church.

Care and support

Try to make sure people are cared for. Time spent at each meeting allowing people to unwind, get something off their chest or refer back to something that was discussed last week, is not time wasted. People need to feel they belong. Many people come to groups like this leaving behind them stressful situations at home or at work. Do not expect them to switch automatically on to our agenda. Allow people to bring their own agenda with them.

Remember that leaders are people too! If you are leading one of these Growth courses, whether you are ordained or lay, you will need some support, feedback and encouragement in that task. Having one or two people who will share in the leadership of the group and can encourage one another will help. So does being linked with and meeting regularly with the clergy and local church leaders. You do not need a lot of initial training to lead an *Emmaus* Growth course. But you do need a good level of ongoing support to be sustained in this ministry.

3   The practical maintenance of the group

Timing

Try to start and finish on time. The notes on timing in the tables assume a session of between one-and-a-half and one-and-three-quarter hours. With a cup of coffee we are therefore talking about a two-hour meeting. Even if some people want to stay on longer than this, make sure it is OK to leave when the two hours are up. If people are experiencing stress at home about attending such a course, it is really important to keep to the deal about how long each session lasts.

You may well find, particularly with a relaxed and participative group, that there is more material given than you have time to work through. On the one hand, it is important not to let the group ramble on, or for talkative people to talk too much. On the other hand, it is good to leave people feeling they could have gone on longer – and wanting more. Do not be afraid to adjust the amount of material you use to fit with your group – though make sure that the prayer/meditation time is not squeezed out.

Venue

Find the best venue for the meeting. For these courses this will probably be somebody's home. But it might not be. Choose somewhere that is warm, comfortable and easy for everyone to get to.

Make sure there is enough seating and that the chairs are comfortable. Make sure that the chairs are arranged in such a way that no one feels excluded.

The handouts

As well as the leaders' guide, this book contains photocopy masters for handouts for each Growth course. These are also available to download from the CD-ROM. You are entitled to make copies of or to download these pages for members of groups in your own church and the book is designed with this in mind. There is one main handout for every session of the course with some optional supplementary sheets.

Most groups will welcome the handouts and find them a valuable summary of each session. We suggest you provide everyone with a simple A4 ring binder to keep them in from week to week. It may help if the leader buys a hole-punch and supplies the sheets ready to slip into the file.

Some groups, however, will be 'paper-resistant' and may be thrown by having too many photocopied sheets to read and keep from week to week. Each course will work without handouts. You may need to provide scrap paper for some of the exercises and to reduce the teaching content in some of the sessions. Don't be afraid to go with the flow of the group and adapt the material to your own needs. That's what it's for.

If people need pencils, paper, Bibles, etc., make sure they know about this beforehand. Whenever possible, make sure you have spares with you for those who forget. Any other materials you will need for a particular session are clearly marked in the leaders' notes.

Coffee

Decide beforehand when you are going to have refreshments. Most groups have tea or coffee at the beginning or the end (or both!), but having refreshments at the beginning often means starting quite late and is therefore an invitation to arrive late! Having refreshments at the end can make the end of the meeting unclear and therefore make it hard for people to leave. You have to make your own decision on this, but how about refreshments in the middle? All the sessions call for some sort of group discussion. Why not set people to work on something, take orders for tea and coffee, and then give them their drinks in their groups? This does help time management.

Having a coffee break also offers the opportunity for the more relaxed, personal conversation that may prove vital in a person's faith journey.

These practical tasks of maintenance are very important. They can make or break a group. You may want to give this responsibility to someone else. The group leader often has enough to worry about without also having to remember to buy the biscuits. You could ask someone to be the host for the group. This person could then be responsible for all these matters. Or have a co-leader who could learn about leading groups by working alongside the leader and taking charge of the practicalities.

4   Praying together

Prayer together is central to Christian maturity and central to these Growth courses. In these sessions, prayer is neither a perfunctory nod to God, nor merely a gathering together of what has been explored (though this is important), but it is an integral part of the learning process. If knowledge of God begins with reflection upon experience (ours and the Church's), and if it creates relationship with God which is nurtured by relationship with one another, then prayer must be at the very heart of all our seeking for God. Without prayer there can be no progress in our discipleship.

Give time for prayer in every session. This is clearly marked in the leaders' notes, but experience shows that sometimes it is the first thing to be squeezed out when time is short. Relegating prayer to the sidelines is the worst possible example of how to grow in discipleship.

Be bold in trying out the variety of methods of prayer which are suggested for these sessions. There is so much to be learned from the rich mosaic of Christian traditions. *Emmaus*, because it does not come from any one churchmanship tradition, aims to help people enter into a rich experience of Christian spirituality. More than anything else this will help people grow in their faith.

There are two great traditions of prayer in the Christian Church, liturgical and spontaneous. Both have proved of enduring value. It is good to build both into the prayer life of groups.

Liturgical prayer

As far as liturgical prayer is concerned, there are not only the services of Morning and Evening Prayer in *Common Worship* but there are also a growing number of versions of Compline (night prayer), and of various liturgical resources such as *Common Worship: Daily Prayer*, *New Patterns for Worship*, *Celebrating Common Prayer* and various Celtic resources. Most clergy will have a number of these. You do not have to use any form in its entirety, but from them you can draw appropriate patterns – and develop your own.

The important thing about liturgical prayer is to keep continuity so that people can rest back on the familiarity. Don't change it every week.

Spontaneous prayer

It often seems more difficult to help a group become comfortable with spontaneous prayer. Remember that no group, or person, is comfortable with anything until they are used to it; so determine to work through the awkward stage into enjoyment.

In helping people not used to praying out loud to begin to do so, it is important to remember that there are two hurdles most people find difficulty getting over. They are 'Will I get air time?' And 'Can I construct a prayer?'

There are ways we can give people 'air time' when they know they are the only ones allowed to pray at that time. Pass a book (Bible?) around a circle of people. Only the person holding the book can pray out loud. When you have prayed, pass the book on. If you do not want to pray aloud, simply pass the book on; but this is your chance.

There are ways of diminishing the sentence construction problem. Rather than saying, 'Let us thank God for his goodness to us by speaking out our praise,' simply say, 'We praise you for . . .' or 'We give thanks for . . .' and add the particular thing for which you want to praise/thank God. In intercession we can invite people to name people or a situation they want to pray for without having to construct a sentence. Because these prayers are single-word, or single-sentence prayers, they also greatly reduce concern about 'air time'.

5 Goals

In the task of leading a group, there are some greater goals that are good to keep in mind, and some specific options which are worth discussing with the leader of the local church. These additional goals are as follows.

Building community

We live in a world that is deeply fragmented, as much through social mobility as by the media, the telephone (and internet) and the break-up of families. People are looking to belong, but are wary of commitment and of being organized or controlled. The Church has a great gift to give such a society. That gift is the Church itself, if it is living as God intends it to live, namely as an inclusive, empowering, faith community. A group doing the *Emmaus* course can become just that. It is important for the leader to look for ways of encouraging such an open and loving community to emerge through doing this course.

Building an engaging community

We follow Jesus Christ as Lord. He revealed himself as the incarnate one, the one who came into our world and lived his life among us, revealing God in the process. Any community that regards itself as Christian will, like Jesus Christ, also be engaged with the world around it. In all our sessions together, making connections with life must be an important goal of the leader. We must be alert to, and seeking to avoid, the danger which Richard Foster highlights in his book, *Prayer*, when he says:

> Many of us today live in a kind of inner apartheid. We segregate out a small corner of pious activities and then can make no spiritual sense out of the rest of our lives.

At every point we need to help the group to make the connection between faith and life. We can do this by:

- *watching our language – checking each other whenever we use unnecessarily religious language ('how would you say that at school, in the supermarket, etc.?' is a good question to ask when we detect this going on);*

- *considering the application ('how would this work out at home/work/in the pub?');*

- *talking about the questions and objections others raise to our faith;*

- *looking for ways of demonstrating our faith (offering to pray for those in need, holding a party or prayer vigil for someone or some need, doing a piece of service together).*

Building a worshipping community

One of the great forms of church life over the centuries has been the monastic movement. There are two things in its life of relevance to the building of the Church community today. One is worship, as T. S. Eliot put it:

> There is no life that is not in community,
> And no community not lived in praise of God.
>
> *Choruses from 'The Rock'*

which is why the prayer and worship elements of the group's life are so important. They build Christian community around the knowledge of God. It is important to keep our eye on that, and to look for ways to encourage that relaxed but real focus on God as the true centre of the group. The early chapters of Acts reveal an attractive church that had its life centred in the praise of God (2.11b, 46-47, 23-26, 10.44-46). It is also, of course, where the Emmaus story ends:

> Then they worshipped him and returned to Jerusalem
> with great joy.
>
> *Luke 24.52*

To build community, it is vital to find ways of building the worship of God that are natural and appropriate to that group. It will repay careful and creative preparation.

In discovering appropriate patterns of prayer, symbols and musical contributions, it is good to look for patterns that can be repeated in the personal lives of group members. In this, group prayer and meditation should feed (and build upon) personal prayer.

Building a community lifestyle

The other thing that holds monastic orders together is their shared 'rule of life' – a commitment to practise certain things in a way that binds people together. The word 'rule' may not be a very helpful one today. A more helpful word, one that fits well with the whole concept of *Emmaus*, is 'way', as in the phrase 'a way of life', or 'lifestyle'. It can be a great help in building a faith community to develop together a specific way of life. Here is one such 'way of life' or 'shared lifestyle' that might emerge out of an *Emmaus* group:

We seek to follow Jesus Christ, by:

- *making time to pray and meditate on God's word to us;*

- *seeking to bless all whose lives we touch each day;*

- *caring for each other in the group beyond our meeting times;*

- *letting our faith affect the whole of our living.*

To sustain such a group lifestyle it would be important to meet regularly (once a month?), and honestly report successes, failures and next steps about our practice of this way of life.

It would be good to clarify with the church leader and with the group, whether – in the duration of this series of courses – there is a commitment to develop such a shared lifestyle. If you do, it will very likely grow out of the action sections at the end of each meeting, and will affect the way that you handle those parts of the programme.

In developing such a shared way of life it is good to remember the following points:

■   *Keep it to not more than half-a-dozen points (three to five is better).*

■   *Keep it as specific as possible.*

■   *Make it memorable (which will include making it as brief as possible).*

■   *Make the way you handle it a gift, not a drag or way of making people feel guilty.*

Leading a group of people who are seeking to grow in Christian faith can be in turns a daunting, stretching, frustrating, exciting, life-giving and joy-building experience. Each person who forms part of an *Emmaus* Growth group is infinitely precious to God. The task of guiding such a group is one of the great privileges of Christian life and ministry. It may sometimes seem an impossible thing for anyone to do well. But the God who calls us also equips us for the task, and to him be the glory.

What's new in the second edition?

We have taken the opportunity of this second edition to make the following changes:

■   *Drawing on experience of the first edition, the text has been simplified in places.*

■   *Many of the handouts have been reduced to two sheets of A4 for easier photocopying. They are also available to download from the CD-ROM.*

■   *Page numbers have been removed from the members' handouts for churches who want to tackle the sessions in a different order.*

■   *The 'Called into life' module has been reduced from five to four sessions.*

■   *Extracts from the Alternative Service Book have been replaced with their equivalents from Common Worship. However, it remains very easy to adapt the handouts to the needs of different churches.*

■   *All Bible quotations are now from the NRSV, the version which is now used across the Emmaus materials.*

Key to icons used in the leaders' notes and members' handouts

 Introduction to the session

 Example timings for the session

 Action replay/reporting back

 Material for reflection

 Buzz groups

 Suggestions for prayer

 Bible study

 Putting it into practice

 Input and discussion

 Module

part 1

Living images

Introduction

Aim

The purpose of this part of *Emmaus* is to help people reflect on what the Bible and Christian tradition teach us about what it means to be fully human, fully alive. Based on Genesis 1, the story of creation, the course explores four aspects of our being human in the sense of our living to the full potential of who we are as those made in the image of God.

Content

The first session explores the dynamic of grace, that is, how God's goodness surrounds and shapes and makes possible our whole lives. In response to this, we are called to walk in thanksgiving.

The second session looks at celebration as a major characteristic of God, heaven and thus, also, of God's purposes for human life.

The third session considers how we are made to be creative in the whole of life, and how we are to do this out of relationship with God – not in our own energy and insights.

The fourth session addresses the issue of our being in community, with God by faith, with others in the fellowship of the Church, and with all humanity because we are made in the image of the Three-persons-in-one-God.

Process

In view of the subject of this course, it is particularly important that the whole life of the group actually demonstrates – rather than undermines – the discovery of the truth that God has set his love upon us and made us his children.

It is therefore important that the themes of grace, thanksgiving, celebration, community and creativity are handled well – and practised – throughout this course.

Look for creative ways of exploring the subject, including having some social event or celebration as part of it, taking time to help the group discover each member's major area of creativity in life and building a community in the group.

Two, contrasting, books that can help in preparing to lead this course are *What's so amazing about grace?* by Philip Yancey and *Learning to Dance* by Michael Mayne.

Session One: What a wonderful world!

	mins
Welcome and introduction	10
Opening prayer	5
Input and discussion: The gift of life	15
Sharing together: What a wonderful world	15
Bible study: Genesis 1.26-31	20
Input and discussion: The goodness of God	10
Prayer together: Thanksgiving	10
Putting it into practice	5

Session Two: Enjoying God's world

	mins
Welcome and opening prayer	5
Action replay	15
Input and discussion: Work and play	20
Sharing together: Sabbath	10
Bible study: Deuteronomy 14.22-27	20
Prayer together	10
Putting it into practice	10

Session Three: Creating with God

	mins
Welcome and opening prayer	5
Action replay	15
Input and discussion: Co-creators with God	10
Sharing together: Our creativity	20
Bible study: 1 Chronicles 29.1-13	15
Prayer together	10
Putting it into practice	15

Session Four: Living with God

	mins
Opening prayer	5
Action replay	10
Input: Made for community	10
Sharing together: Finding identity	15
Input and discussion: God is community	10
Bible study: Luke 1.39-45	20
Prayer together	10
Putting it into practice	10

What a wonderful world!

Welcome and introduction

If this is a group that has been meeting before, the introduction can be kept to a minimum. However, do remember that changing a group even by the addition of one person makes the group into a new one. In that case, or if this is a new group, then it is good to take time in this first session to introduce ourselves to each other.

As the subject for this session is the wonder of God's world, it would be good to get people to share their favourite holiday place, or the most beautiful place in the world or the most memorable view they have ever seen. Make sure they are encouraged to say how this affected them and why it was special.

Opening prayer

After everyone has had a chance to speak, one of the group should lead the opening prayers. It is good if a different member of the group can lead each session. Give plenty of warning and help where necessary.

The idea for this time of prayer is simply to put us back in touch with a sense of wonder at the created world. Try one of the following ideas:

- *Get hold of a poster-sized picture of the earth from the moon.*

- *Display a picture of a beautiful scene (preferably without religious words on it!).*

- *Play Louis Armstrong's rendering of 'What a wonderful world'.*

- *Creative members of the group, either this week or in future weeks, may want to make a tape/slide, or other, visual/musical presentation.*

- *Read Psalm 8 to the group.*

Thank God for the wonder of his world and ask for his presence as you meet together.

Input and discussion: The gift of life

Ask the group to reflect in twos and threes for a few minutes on the question:

'If you were to sum up the whole meaning of life in just a few words – what would you say?'

Take a few moments to listen to one another's answers. Then introduce the course and the central idea for this session around the following points:

- *One way Christians would sum up the whole meaning of life is 'gift'.*

- *The key phrase in Scripture that means gift is 'grace'.*

- *Life is a gift from God, a gift to be enjoyed.*

■ *Remember that life was given to us, we did not ask for it or earn it. Equally the air we breathe, the water we drink, the seeds we sow, are all – at least originally – 'givens' in life.*

Point out how much we 'take for granted' and think together about what those things are. Reflect on the phrase 'taking life for granted'.

How does that make life different from when it is 'received by faith'?

What difference does the idea make to the way we live?

Sharing together: What a wonderful world

Construct a list of your own group's 'seven wonders of the world'. Encourage people to spend time hearing about each other's wonders. Either do this all together or, if you are leading a large group, split into smaller units. Each of the smaller groups can then share their list with the others.

Bible study: Genesis 1.26-31

Ask someone to read out the passage.

Give a brief introduction to the beginning of Genesis. Don't get sidetracked by the issues of how it is true – but you may need to deal briefly with the question, particularly if it is a major stumbling block for some members of the group.

A story to help deal with this is about an electrician and a bus driver at a set of traffic lights. When asked 'why are the lights red' the electrician gives an impressive technical explanation of how electricity travels along the wire to the bulb, which heats up and gives out light as well as heat. The glass of the light acts as a filter and cuts out all colours of the spectrum, except red. That is why the light is red. When the bus driver is asked the question he says 'Because I've got to stop'. He has actually given the better answer. He has told us 'why' the lights are red, not 'how'; and by his answer he has told us that someone has put the lights there for a purpose. Genesis is like the bus driver.

Get the group to talk about what they think it means to be made in the image of God.

Draw out the aspects of God's nature that we share such as:

■ *rational thought;*

■ *moral consciousness;*

■ *creativity;*

■ *love;*

■ *relationship . . . and much more.*

Input and discussion: The goodness of God

Without looking at the sheet, ask the group to think together, and to write down, the different ways in which God's grace and goodness come to us.

Draw out the following points in the discussion:

God's goodness comes to us through:

■ *Creation: the wonder and beauty of the world, our own bodies and faculties.*

■ *Relationships: family, friends and places where we work, worship, love, belong.*

- *Experiences: the many stages of life, and the present phase we are living in.*
- *Gospel: the knowledge of God and his love for us.*

Prayer together: Thanksgiving

We respond to God with thanksgiving. Gather together the thoughts and concerns of the meeting in your own words. If the group is happy with praying aloud, ask each person to express their own thanksgiving in their own words.

Groups less familiar with extemporary prayer may find it helpful just to name the things for which they want to give thanks to God (e.g. 'friends', 'holidays', 'music', 'barbecues', etc.) with someone concluding with an expression of thanks to God for all that has been named.

Then pray together the Psalm on the members' handout, or a prayer such as the Anglican prayer known as the General Thanksgiving, or other thanksgivings (see pages 48–56 of *Common Worship*). These are printed on the members' handouts.

Putting it into practice

How can we develop our sense of wonder? What practical steps can we take to be wonder-full people?! Agree together some things you can do as a group this week – perhaps bringing one object, photograph or piece of music back to the group next time to sum up what you have discovered.

Remember, the heart of the Church's life is the Eucharist, which is the Greek word for thanksgiving. How could the communion services at our church give better expression to our thanksgiving? How can we express thankfulness to God in the whole of our living? How can we deal with the busy-ness that robs us of the time to stop, wonder and give thanks? How can we express thanks and appreciation to close friends and to people we meet in the course of each day?

Summary and example timings

	mins
Welcome and introduction	10
Opening prayer	5
Input and discussion: The gift of life	15
Sharing together: What a wonderful world	15
Bible study: Genesis 1.26-31	20
Input and discussion: The goodness of God	10
Prayer together: Thanksgiving	10
Putting it into practice	5

What a wonderful world!

Input and discussion: The gift of life

> [Jesus said]: I came that they may have life, and have it abundantly.
>
> John. 10.10

The Bible is like the Maker's Handbook. In it people are described as 'living images' of God. That likeness to God is to be lived out every day, for life is a gift to be enjoyed, not a problem to be solved.

Sharing together: What a wonderful world

Think back to moments of wonder in your childhood, to see what they have to say about how we can get in touch with the goodness of God and his gift of life.

Construct your own list of 'the seven wonders of the world'.

One of the reasons that Jesus put a child among his disciples and said 'unless you change and become like children, you will never enter the kingdom of heaven', (Matthew 18.1-4) was because children have a great capacity to enjoy what is, to be full of wonder, to take delight in little things. It is this capacity to be fully alive that God comes to restore in even the most broken and cynical among us. We are to let him restore to us 'the joy of our salvation'.

Bible study: Genesis 1.26-31

While science can often tell us how the world is made, the focus of Genesis (and the whole Bible) is on *why* God made the world.

> Then God said, 'Let us make humankind in our image, according to our likeness; and let them have dominion over the fish of the sea, and over the birds of the air, and over the cattle, and over all the wild animals of the earth, and over every creeping thing that creeps upon the earth.'
>
> > So God created humankind in his image,
> > in the image of God he created them;
> > male and female he created them.
>
> God blessed them, and God said to them, 'Be fruitful and multiply, and fill the earth and subdue it; and have dominion over the fish of the sea and over the birds of the air and over every living thing that moves upon the earth.' God said, 'See, I have given you every plant yielding seed that is upon the face of all the earth, and every tree with seed in its fruit; you shall have them for food. And to every beast of the earth, and to every bird of the air, and to everything that creeps on the earth, everything that has the breath of life, I have given every green plant for food.' And it was so. God saw everything that he had made, and indeed, it was very good. And there was evening and there was morning, the sixth day.
>
> Genesis 1.26-31

Prayer together: Thanksgiving

Psalm 103

Bless the Lord, O my soul,
and all that is within me,
bless his holy name.
Bless the Lord, O my soul,
and do not forget all his benefits –
who forgives all your iniquity,
who heals all your diseases,
who redeems your life from the Pit,
who crowns you with steadfast love and mercy,
who satisfies you with good as long as you live
so that your youth is renewed like the eagle's.

Psalm 103.1-5

Without affirmation it is hard to live well.

Henri Nouwen, *Life of the Beloved*

Putting it into practice

How can we develop our sense of wonder? What practical steps can we take to be wonder-full people?! Remember, the heart of the Church's life is the Eucharist, which is the Greek word for thanksgiving. That needs to be expressed to others as well as to God.

Enjoying God's world

Welcome and opening prayer

Invite someone in the group to lead this part of the meeting, but make sure you give them plenty of warning and help if necessary.

Action replay

Changing the way we live is the goal of this module of Living images. This means that 'getting in touch with each other and the subject' is very vital.

It is important not to think 'we did thanksgiving last week', but rather to take all four weeks to return to that subject and talk about successes and obstacles.

Get the group to work on the issues raised: resist the temptation to be the fount of all wisdom – none of us is!

How did we get on with practising the things we agreed to try out last week?

■   *Does anyone have good news to report on this front? Tell us about it.*

■   *Did anyone find it more difficult than they expected? What were the obstacles?*

Our aim throughout these weeks is to develop these skills. Now is the time to agree how we want to develop our ability to live in and express the wonder of God's gift of life to us.

Input and discussion: Work and play

Western Christianity has always seen humanity as the climax of creation (Genesis 1. 26 – 2.3). The Protestant work ethic (our having dominion) has been the result. It has profoundly shaped the society in which we live, not least in the development of science, industry and technology. It has given us great gains but created major problems too.

What have been the gains?

As a group, compile a list of some of the greatest gains from the development of science and technology.

What major problems have been created?

As a group, compile a list of the biggest problems that have been caused by our acting as if we had dominion over creation and could use the creation in whichever way we pleased.

Sharing together: Sabbath

Although Genesis 1 ends on day six (our having dominion), the creation story ends on day seven, which gives a very different picture – namely of God enjoying his creation.

> Thus the heavens and the earth were finished, and all their multitude. And on the seventh day God finished the work that he had done, and he rested on the seventh day from all the work that he had done. So God blessed the seventh day and hallowed it, because on it God rested from all the work that he had done in creation.
>
> Genesis 2.1-3

In our culture today people are either overworked or out of work. Maybe what we now need is a Protestant play ethic. This is what we are looking at in this session. How we can reflect God's character (image) by being those who take time to stop and enjoy what is, what has been given us, and the life we have.

In other words, how we can enjoy Sabbath: the gift of rest and re-creation (including 'charging our batteries'). Here are three questions:

1   Why is our culture so bad at stopping and enjoying what is, rather than getting or achieving more?

2   When we do try to 'enjoy ourselves', why does it so often end up in overdoing (food, drink, etc.) or in numbing out (in front of the TV)? Is there a better way?

3   What have been the two most enjoyable experiences in our lives in recent years?

These questions are printed on the members' handout. As a whole group, or in twos and threes, get people to share together their responses to these questions.

Bible study: Deuteronomy 14.22-27

Learning from God's people

The Jewish people have always been skilled at celebrations. We are going to look at the instructions they were given, and see what we can learn from them about how we can develop the art of stopping and enjoying all that is.

What strikes you about what they did and did not do?

Who was present?

What can we learn from them for today?

Ask the different groups to share with one another what they have learned.

Prayer together

Light a candle and thank God for the gift of light, and the flickering light of our lives.

Read Proverbs 8.22-31 (play quiet music in the background?).

(Sing a song or hymn if you wish.)

Spend some time in silence. It is important in this session just to stop and let people reflect.

End by saying together this prayer:

> Almighty God,
> who wonderfully created us in your own image
> and yet more wonderfully restored us
> through your Son Jesus Christ:
> grant that, as he came to share in our humanity,
> so we may share the life of his divinity;
> who is alive and reigns with you,
> in the unity of the Holy Spirit,
> one God, now and for ever. Amen.
>
> *Common Worship*: Collect for the First Sunday of Christmas

Putting it into practice

Decide together how to take forward the things that were worked on during the action replay at the start of the session; and how we can – as individuals, families, a group (or as part of the local church or community) – act on what we have explored since.

Is there some celebration we could plan as part of the life of this group that would express the insights we have gained in this session? Going out together somewhere, doing something together, creating an event to celebrate something?

We need to remember that celebration includes:

- *worshipping God;*

- *enjoying creation;*

- *enjoying human creativity (art, architecture, sport, etc.);*

- *stopping, looking, contemplating;*

- *shouting, dancing, singing;*

- *doing any or all of the above, with others.*

Summary and example timings

	mins
Welcome and opening prayer	5
Action replay	15
Input and discussion: Work and play	20
Sharing together: Sabbath	10
Bible study: Deuteronomy 14.22-27	20
Prayer together	10
Putting it into practice	10

Enjoying God's world

Sharing together: Sabbath

God likes life, he invented it!

1   Why are we bad at stopping and enjoying what is, rather than getting or achieving more?

2   When we do try to 'enjoy ourselves', why does it so often end up in overdoing (food, drink, etc.), or in 'numbing out' in front of the TV? Why? Is there a better way?

3   What have been the two most enjoyable experiences in our lives in recent years? Why?

Bible study: Deuteronomy 14.22-27

Learning from God's people

The Jewish people have always been skilled at celebrations. This passage contains some surprising instructions about 'tithing' (giving a tenth). Our word 'holiday' comes from the word 'holy-day'. Here the children of Israel show us how to put worship, fellowship, care for the needy and enjoyment together as one whole event.

> Set apart a tithe of all the yield of your seed that is brought in yearly from the field. In the presence of the Lord your God, in the place that he will choose as a dwelling for his name, you shall eat the tithe of your grain, your wine, and your oil, as well as the firstlings of your herd and flock, so that you may learn to fear the Lord your God always. But if, when the Lord your God has blessed you, the distance is so great that you are unable to transport it, because the place where the Lord your God will choose to set his name is too far away from you, then you may turn it into money. With the money secure in hand, go to the place that the Lord your God will choose; spend the money for whatever you wish – oxen, sheep, wine, strong drink, or whatever you desire. And you shall eat there in the presence of the Lord your God, you and your household rejoicing together. As for the Levites resident in your towns, do not neglect them, because they have no allotment or inheritance with you.
>
> Deuteronomy 14.22-27

What strikes you about what they did and did not do?

Who was present?

What can we learn from them for today?

Prayer together

Almighty God,
who wonderfully created us in your own image
and yet more wonderfully restored us
through your Son Jesus Christ:
grant that, as he came to share in our humanity,
so we may share the life of his divinity;
who is alive and reigns with you,
in the unity of the Holy Spirit,
one God, now and for ever. Amen.

Common Worship: Collect for the First Sunday of Christmas

Putting it into practice

We need to remember that celebration includes:

- *worshipping God;*

- *enjoying creation;*

- *enjoying human creativity (art, architecture, sport, etc.);*

- *stopping, looking, contemplating;*

- *shouting, dancing, singing;*

- *doing any or all of the above, with others.*

Something to ponder

How to enjoy yourself – don't!

We actually enjoy ourselves most when we are enjoying someone or something else.

- So worship is not really about enjoying ourselves but about enjoying God.

- Going on holiday, or out into the country, is about enjoying the scenery and colour, etc.

- Going to the theatre, or cinema, is about enjoying human culture and skills.

- Playing sport, or a musical instrument, is about enjoying making things with others.

We come to know even ourselves, not through turning inward to study and analyse, but by turning outward to love all that is real and other than ourselves.

Leanne Payne, *The Healing Presence*

Once every day I shall simply stare at a tree, a flower, a cloud, or a person. I shall not then be concerned at all to ask what they are but simply be glad that they are.

Dr Clyde Kirby (quoted in Leanne Payne)

Creating with God

Welcome and opening prayer

As with each session of the course, it is good if one of the group can lead this, but make sure you give them plenty of warning and help if necessary. Encourage people to be creative and to be themselves.

Action replay

How have we been getting on with walking in thanksgiving, and with learning to take time to stop and enjoy God, life, others and creation?

The goal is to let the gospel shape our attitude to life and our lifestyle.

■ *What is our good news?*

■ *What are the obstacles?*

■ *How can we help each other take another step forward?*

You may need more time for this, which is great. Allow people the opportunity to share their feelings and do not worry if other timings are affected. Once groups begin to 'form' into real communities, barriers come down and people become more real, honest and vocal. Conflicts sometimes emerge but are usually a sign of life rather than death.

Input and discussion: Co-creators with God

In the first session, we considered life as a gift to be received with thanksgiving. When we do that we acknowledge that we are creatures before the Creator, which is a primary mark of living as images of God. The only alternative is to live as if we were God, complete in ourselves.

> Sin is our determination to manage by ourselves.
>
> Rudolf Bultmann, quoted in G. Quell et al., *Sin*

In the second session we thought about the climax of creation as being the seventh day, when God celebrated and enjoyed what he had made.

In this session we are going to explore the most obvious ways in which we are made in the image of God – namely that we are creators, indeed co-creators with him.

We need to allow God to be Lord of the whole of life. Our creativity involves many things:

■ *relationships;*

■ *work;*

■ *bringing children into the world, and bringing them up before God;*

- *artistic work;*

- *hobbies;*

- *political action, and anything else that we do.*

Make sure your discussion is that wide. You may want to make a poster or a list of different areas of creativity. Creativity is more than church work. God's concern is with the 'ministry of work' not just 'the work of ministry'.

Sharing together: Our creativity

In small groups ask yourselves these questions:

What are our earliest experiences of making things in childhood?

What did we like to create? Not just things but events. How did we play?

What are some of the most significant and enjoyable things that we feel we have made?

Can we identify ways in which God was present in that creative work?

What is the main area of our creativity today:

- *as primary responsibility;*

- *as leisure activity;*

- *in relationships?*

What connection does God want to have with these areas?

Bible study: 1 Chronicles 29.1-13

Read the passage aloud.

Help the group to identify what David was creating physically, socially and spiritually.

Draw out the group's own response to the Scripture. Only use the list below if they get stuck:

- *a community of people who shared his vision and were eager to honour God and willing to sacrifice to that end;*

- *a vision;*

- *motivation of a whole community that would outlive him;*

- *an example to follow;*

- *the practical resources for a piece of physical work (temple-building);*

- *a group of people who would see it through;*

- *faith in God and thankfulness for his goodness;*

- *a community motivated by faith and grace.*

(Not bad for one day's work!)

How does all this apply to our experience of life today?

Point out that, in our own creativity, we are often working on a number of different levels, like David (physical, social, emotional, spiritual).

Prayer together

As with the other times of prayer, try to get people to be relaxed. Use music, and symbols – a lighted candle, a memorable picture, a flower, an icon, etc. – if that will be helpful for the group. Slow the pace down by all possible means. If you are getting someone else to do this (a good principle) make sure that you give them enough warning, enough support, help and advice, enough space (to do it their own – creative – way), and enough feedback afterwards so that they feel valued, and can learn.

Light a candle, read Psalm 8 and give thanks for the creative work of each one of us.

End with the prayer:

> Let the favour of the Lord our God be upon us,
> and prosper for us the work of our hands –
> O prosper the work of our hands!
>
> Psalm 90.17

Putting it into practice

One of the special pieces of work that God calls all Christians to be involved in through their baptism is the priesthood of all believers, for we are a priestly people. This means that he calls us to bless others, his creation, and the work in which we are all involved.

How can we bless each other in our work this week?

In groups of two or three share the major focus of our creative efforts in the coming week, and pray for one another in the way we are accustomed to as a group. Conclude the time by putting God's blessing on each other by saying:

> The Lord bless you and keep you;
> the Lord make his face to shine upon you, and be gracious to you;
> the Lord lift up his countenance upon you, and give you peace.
> Now and always. Amen.
>
> Numbers 6.24-26

Summary and example timings

	mins
Welcome and opening prayer	5
Action replay	15
Input and discussion: Co-creators with God	10
Sharing together: Our creativity	20
Bible study: 1 Chronicles 29.1-13	15
Prayer together	10
Putting it into practice	15

Creating with God

Input and discussion: Co-creators with God

Creativity is much wider than 'church work', though it can include it. God created, takes delight in, and is engaged in redeeming all that is. His concern is not only for 'the work of ministry'; but also for 'the ministry of work'.

Sharing together: Our creativity

Share together your earliest experiences of making things in our childhood.

- *What did you like to create? (Not only things, but events and anything else that comes to mind.)*

- *What are some of the most significant/enjoyable things that you feel you have made/created in your life so far?*

- *Can you identify ways in which God was present in that creative work?*

What is the main area of our creativity today:

- *as primary responsibility;*

- *as leisure activity;*

- *in relationships?*

What connection does God want to have with these areas?

Bible study: 1 Chronicles 29.1-13

As this is read try to identify what it is that David was creating.

King David said to the whole assembly, 'My son Solomon, whom alone God has chosen, is young and inexperienced, and the work is great; for the temple will not be for mortals but for the Lord God. So I have provided for the house of my God, so far as I was able, the gold for the things of gold, the silver for the things of silver, and the bronze for the things of bronze, the iron for the things of iron, and wood for the things of wood, besides great quantities of onyx and stones for setting, antimony, coloured stones, all sorts of precious stones, and marble in abundance. Moreover, in addition to all that I have provided for the holy house, I have a treasure of my own of gold and silver, and because of my devotion to the house of my God I give it to the house of my God: three thousand talents of gold, of the gold of Ophir, and seven thousand talents of refined silver, for overlaying the walls of the house, and for all the work to be done by artisans, gold for the things of gold and silver for the things of silver. Who then will offer willingly, consecrating themselves today to the Lord?'

Then the leaders of ancestral houses made their freewill offerings, as did also the leaders of the tribes, the commanders of the thousands and of the hundreds, and the officers over the king's work. They gave for the service of the house of God five thousand talents and ten thousand darics of gold, ten thousand talents of silver, eighteen thousand talents of bronze, and one hundred thousand talents of iron. Whoever had precious stones gave them to the treasury of the house of the Lord, into the care of Jehiel the Gershonite. Then the people rejoiced because these had given willingly, for with single mind they had offered freely to the Lord; King David also rejoiced greatly.

Then David blessed the Lord in the presence of all the assembly; David said: 'Blessed are you, O Lord, the God of our ancestor Israel, forever and ever. Yours, O Lord, are the greatness, the power, the glory, the victory, and the majesty; for all that is in the heavens and on the earth is yours; yours is the kingdom, O Lord, and you are exalted as head above all. Riches and honour come from you, and you rule over all. In your hand are power and might; and it is in your hand to make great and to give strength to all. And now, our God, we give thanks to you and praise your glorious name.

1 Chronicles 29.1-13

Prayer together

Light a candle, read Psalm 8 and give thanks to God for his work of creation and give thanks for the creative work of each one of us.

End with the prayer:

> Let the favour of the Lord our God be upon us,
> and prosper for us the work of our hands –
> O prosper the work of our hands!
>
> Psalm 90.17

Putting it into practice

Through our baptism God calls all Christians to be involved in a special piece of work – being part of the priesthood of all believers. This is about blessing God's world and the people in it – including each other. Equally we are called to bless God's creation and to bless the work in which we are involved. As we lift various situations, needs and people before God we can pray:

> The Lord bless you and keep you;
> the Lord make his face to shine upon you, and be gracious to you;
> the Lord lift up his countenance upon you, and give you peace.
> Now and always. Amen.
>
> Numbers 6.24-26

Living with God

Opening prayer

It is good if one of the group can lead this, but make sure you give them plenty of warning and help if necessary. Encourage the group to enjoy the prayer and to be creative. Perhaps the person leading could show or describe something they have created in the past.

Action replay

How have we been getting on with:

1   Walking in thanksgiving?

2   Enjoying the gift of God, life, others and creation?

3   Being creative and blessing others?

Remember, the goal is to let the gospel shape our attitude to life and our lifestyle.

■   *What is our good news?*

■   *What are the obstacles?*

■   *How can we help each other take another step forward?*

Input: Made for community

Remind the group of what you have covered so far.
(This material is on the members' handout.)

So far in this module on 'Living images' we have thought about:

■   *life as a gift to be received with thanksgiving (session one);*

■   *the Sabbath (seventh day) as the climax of creation (session two);*

■   *ourselves as creators, indeed co-creators with God (session three).*

Now we will explore the way in which, because we are made in God's image, we are made for community: we are social beings.

Give the group opportunity to say what they have grasped so far as a result of working together on this material.

Sharing together: Finding identity

In groups of two or three, talk about the people who have been the greatest influence on us and our ability to accept ourselves: parents, siblings, school friends, teachers, relatives, saints, media personalities . . . whoever. How have they shaped who we are or what we aspire to be?

Input and discussion: God is community

This being-in-relationship is seen, by Christians, as stemming from the nature of God as Trinity. God is a community; a network of loving, affirming, relationships, who are distinct as persons, yet one in will and love. To be made in God's image, inevitably means, therefore, that we are made for community.

> There is no life that is not in community,
> And no community not lived in praise of God.
>
> T. S. Eliot, *Choruses from 'The Rock'*

There are two sides to human relationships:

1   Identity: what makes me different from you.

2   Intimacy: what makes me one with you.

We need both. Indeed, having a relationship is learning to flow between these two poles – being ourselves and being with others. Explain this to people and then get them to share with their neighbour which one they find easier and which one more difficult – identity or intimacy; being myself or being with others.

As a whole group, discuss together your experience of finding identity in community.

There are some quotations in the group members' handout at this point. Draw attention to them, as they will underline the important point that is being made here.

Bible study: Luke 1.39-45

Questions to explore

■   *What on earth is happening here?*

■   *What does that say to us in our relationships today?*

Points to draw out

■   *The ordinariness of the situation: two pregnant woman – cousins – talking together.*

■   *The extra-ordinariness of the situation: one not married, the other past the years of child-bearing.*

■   *A mutual experience of give and take: neither has all the answers.*

■   *Finding God in the midst of life: they were nowhere near a church but they were 'church' – two or three meeting in the name of Christ.*

■   *Listening was a vital part of what they gave each other.*

Additionally (if there is enough time)

Get people to read out loud some, or all, of the following verses and, after each one, invite people to say what authority God has given us for the work he has called us to:

■   *Matthew 28.18-20*

■   *Romans 12.2*

■   *Colossians 2.9-10*

- *Colossians 3.12*

- *1 Peter 1.2*

- *1 Peter 2.9.*

Prayer together

Follow the usual pattern, getting people to relax by using music and symbols where appropriate and slowing the pace down.

If you are getting someone else to lead the prayer make sure you give them enough warning and enough support, help and advice. Also enough space to do it in their own – creative – way, and enough feedback afterwards so that they feel valued and can learn.

Make sure you include in this session prayers for one another, so that we may live out, and live in, the truths we have studied.

Putting it into practice

Encourage people to reflect on what spoke to us and what we have most valued about this course on Living images. Decide how to continue living out the things we have been discovering and learning together. It is important to find ways to allow this material to have a lasting effect on the lives of group members and the dynamic of the group. Work out together how this can be so. For example, would it be helpful to review from time to time as a group how we are progressing in thanksgiving, celebrating, creating, and blessing/affirming others? Obviously much more is possible if the group is to continue in existence after the end of this course.

Summary and example timings

	mins
Opening prayer	5
Action replay	10
Input: Made for community	10
Sharing together: Finding identity	15
Input and discussion: God is community	10
Bible study: Luke 1.39-45	20
Prayer together	10
Putting it into practice	10

Living with God

Input: Made for community

So far in this module on Living images, we have thought about:

■　*life as a gift to be received with thanksgiving (session one);*

■　*the Sabbath (seventh day) as the climax of creation (session two);*

■　*ourselves as creators, indeed co-creators with God (session three).*

Now we will explore the way in which, because we are made in God's image, we are made for community: we are social beings.

Essentially we are beings-in-relationship. Our identity comes not simply from within, but through relationships. This is why modern people often struggle with their sense of identity, because they have a limited and fragmented sense of belonging anywhere.

Sharing together: Finding identity

Questions to explore

■　*The people who have been the greatest influence on us.*

■　*Those who have most helped us to accept ourselves.*

How have they shaped who we are and what we want to become?

God is community

This being-in-relationship is seen, by Christians, as stemming from the nature of God as Trinity. God is a community; a network of loving, affirming, supportive relationships: distinct persons, yet one in will and love. To be made in God's image inevitably means, therefore, that we are made for community.

> There is no life that is not in community,
> and no community not lived in praise of God.
>
> T. S. Eliot, *Choruses from 'The Rock'*

There are two sides to human relationships – identity and intimacy. Identity is what makes me different from you. Intimacy is what makes me one with you.

We need both. Indeed, having a relationship is learning to flow between these two poles – being ourselves and being with others.

Share together which one you find easier and which one more difficult – identity or intimacy; being yourself or being with others.

Discuss together your experience of being comfortable with yourself when you belong to any group.

Background quotations

These underline the vital points about identity and community that are being made in this session.

The loss of a sense of belonging

> The Consumer Society is a formation system which educates us to a life of fragmented relatedness.
>
> John Kavanaugh, *Still Following Christ in a Consumer Society*

One obstacle to intimacy

> One form of love-destroying dishonesty characteristic of life together in our marriages and our churches is our niceness. In our niceness we believe that being supportive means never speaking our real thoughts and feelings in areas of disagreement.
>
> Roberta Bondi, *To Pray and to Love*

The importance of self-acceptance

> There can be no love of others, much less love of God, where there is no self to do the loving.
>
> Roberta Bondi, *To Pray and to Love*

Bible study: Luke 1.39-45

> In those days Mary set out and went with haste to a Judean town in the hill country, where she entered the house of Zechariah and greeted Elizabeth. When Elizabeth heard Mary's greeting, the child leaped in her womb. And Elizabeth was filled with the Holy Spirit and exclaimed with a loud cry, 'Blessed are you among women, and blessed is the fruit of your womb. And why has this happened to me, that the mother of my Lord comes to me? For as soon as I heard the sound of your greeting, the child in my womb leaped for joy. And blessed is she who believed that there would be a fulfilment of what was spoken to her by the Lord.'
>
> Luke 1.39-45

Questions to explore

■   *What on earth is happening here?*

■   *What does that say to us in our relationships today?*

Prayer together

This will include prayer for one another, that we may live out, and live in, the truths we have studied together.

A Prayer

Almighty God,
in Christ you make all things new:
transform the poverty of our nature by the riches of your grace,
and in the renewal of our lives
make known your heavenly glory;
through Jesus Christ your Son our Lord,
who is alive and reigns with you,
in the unity of the Holy Spirit,
one God, now and for ever. Amen.

Common Worship: Collect for the Second Sunday of Epiphany

Putting it into practice

It is important to find ways to allow this material to have a lasting effect on our lives. It will also affect the life of this group.

Work out together your next steps.

part 7

Overcoming evil

Introduction

This module fits well as a follow-on from the previous one on 'Living images' but works equally well as a stand-alone course.

The subject is sin. This is not an easy or comfortable subject, but one that Scripture and the Christian tradition clearly teach is vital to a wholesome and mature attitude to life. The most obvious dangers and opportunities are set out below. It is helpful to use them as a yardstick by which to measure the way the group is engaging with the subject, and as a checklist to use in preparing for each session.

Aim

The Cross lies at the heart of the Christian faith. It is the means God has chosen to overcome evil. He did not do this by ignoring wrong, or by wiping wrongdoers (us) off the face of the earth. He did so rather by entering our world and fighting evil, but not with the weapons of the world (Ephesians 6.10-20, especially v. 12). It is to this that our baptism commits us – 'to fight valiantly as a disciple of Christ against sin, the world and the devil' (*Common Worship*, p. 354). It is this that Paul continually teaches the Churches he wrote to: see especially Romans 6 and Colossians 3. It is good to keep these two passages in mind throughout this course.

This fighting evil, not with human power or with hatred, but by overcoming it with good, touches the whole of life.

■   *We are to overcome evil in our lives through a proper love of that which is holy, healthy and God-given in us. (See the session on personal identity.)*

■   *We are to overcome evil in the Church through the power of forgiveness.*

■   *We are to overcome evil in human society, and the 'structures of injustice'.*

Two modern examples of this overcoming of evil can be seen in the work of Nelson Mandela and Martin Luther King. They did not preach racial hatred, or bring about change by hating whites, but by preaching and living reconciliation. So Nelson Mandela spoke not of blacks winning over whites, but of South Africa becoming a 'rainbow people' – a telling and literally 'colourful' image by which to overcome racial hostility, from either side.

This course is designed to help members discover how to apply this principle of overcoming evil with good in their lives, homes, churches, communities, country and in creation itself. It is important for leaders to keep their eye on this one goal:

> Do not be overcome by evil, but overcome evil with good.
>
> Romans 12.21

Some things to avoid

There are several things to watch, allow to come to the surface, and deal with.

First, is the romantic approach to sin: namely the notion that 'everyone is lovely underneath', and that it is rather censorious to talk about sin. As the notes say, in the age of gulags and concentration camps, we cannot go along with that attitude.

Second, is the shallow approach, which sees sin simply as some things that a few notorious characters and political leaders indulge in – but not most of us. Hence the oft-repeated remark at funerals, 'he/she never did anyone any harm'.

Third, is the judgemental approach, which sees sin as what other people do. This can be all too frequent in Christian and other religious circles. Watch it and deal with it.

Some outcomes to work for

Why do we need to consider this subject? For the same reason we teach children to avoid touching hot things or eating food that has been on the floor. We can be harmfully affected if we do not know what to avoid and what to fight against. The intended outcome for a group studying this material is that, at the end, they will have:

■ *a clearer grasp of the nature of sin/evil as a distorting force in our individual lives and in the whole of human society;*

■ *a deeper awareness of the presence of addictions and idols even in the lives of those who are followers of Christ;*

■ *a greater ability to connect what the Bible says about sin with our experience of life, particularly in a world where moral values are being questioned and eroded;*

■ *a more mature commitment to overcoming evil with good by taking up the Cross and following Christ's costly mission.*

Some practical suggestions for worship and meditation

Each session opens with prayer and ends with a meditation. It is good to develop some simple pattern for each of these, with sufficient similarity from week to week that people know what to expect and what is coming, and can concentrate on prayer or worship rather than on 'what are we are meant to be doing now?'.

For this reason it may be good to ask one person or two people working together to lead all the opening prayer times, and another one or two people (or possibly the leader) can then handle the closing meditation.

What follows can be used as a framework for such times, or as the raw material out of which the actual pattern can be developed for the local situation.

The opening prayer
This is intended to be a brief focusing on God and stilling of ourselves after a busy day.

I   A word of orientation around God
Read a verse from Scripture such as,

> Be still, and know that I am God!
> I am exalted among the nations,
> I am exalted in the earth.
>
> Psalm 46.10

or

Read part or all of Psalms 91, 92, 93 or 95.

2   An act of stilling ourselves before God

Get people to sit with their hands facing palm downwards on their thighs and use that body language to express releasing to God the concerns, joys, frustrations, unfinished business and regrets of the day – allow one or two minutes of silence.

Then invite people to turn their hands upward and open, as an expression of openness to God and expectancy of his giving us good gifts in our time together – allow one or two minutes of silence.

3   A prayer of openness to God

Either extemporary prayer of invitation for God's presence, or use of some liturgical prayer such as:

> Eternal God and Father,
> you create and redeem us by the power of your love:
> guide and strengthen us by your Spirit,
> that we may give ourselves in love and service
> to one another and to you;
> through Jesus Christ our Lord. Amen.
>
> *Common Worship: Daily Prayer.* Collect for Morning Prayer on Tuesday

Closing meditation

This is intended to gather up our thoughts and allow God the opportunity of underlining any particular truth that has spoken to us. Here is a possible pattern for developing your own.

1   Focus on a Christian symbol

Christian truth is communicated through signs and symbols as much as through words and statements. It is good to select one and use it each week throughout this session. In view of the fact that the subject is sin/evil, it is appropriate to use a symbol that connects with the Cross, the supreme symbol of Christ's overcoming evil with good. The symbol used could be a cross, an icon of Christ on the Cross, a cup or chalice or a candle.

It is helpful to begin the meditation with some such comment as:

-     *(with cross/icon): 'We worship the Lamb of God who takes away the sin of the world'.*

-     *(with a candle): 'We welcome you, Lord Jesus Christ, light in our dark world'.*

Be still/silent or use some calming (choral?) music. The aim is to create an atmosphere of quiet openness and reverence.

2   Reading of a Christian insight

This is in the members' handout for each week and is the variable part of this closing meditation.

3   Quiet reflection

It is helpful to give some guidance, but only by way of a one-sentence comment, such as:

> In the stillness let us allow the Holy Spirit to sharpen our grasp of one insight to take from this session.

Expressing the same thought in words natural to the person leading is better still.

4   Prayer response

If the group is well established, people may well be able to pray spontaneously. If not, it will encourage those less familiar with this form of prayer (and inhibit those who are too talkative in prayer) to say something such as:

Let us express those insights/resolves in single-sentence prayers beginning with words such as 'Thank you, Lord, for . . . ' or 'Lord, help us to . . .'.

As an alternative or concluding response:

> Almighty God,
> we thank you for the gift of your holy word.
> May it be a lantern to our feet,
> a light to our paths,
> and a strength to our lives.
> Take us and use us
> to love and serve
> in the power of the Holy Spirit
> and in the name of your Son,
> Jesus Christ our Lord. Amen.
>
> *Common Worship:* A Prayer of Dedication

Putting it into practice

It is important to be as straightforward as possible with what the group agrees to do. Make it specific, achievable and something for which the group clearly has energy.

Remember to make a note of it, for your own action, and as the material you will need at the start of the next session under 'Action replay'.

Summary and example timings

	mins
Welcome and opening prayer	10
Input and discussion: What is sin?	10
Group exercise: Sin is like . . .	15
Bible study: Romans 1.18-25	25
Sharing together: A redefining moment	10
Meditation	15
Putting it into practice	5

Session Two: Idols and addictions

	mins
Welcome and opening prayer	5
Action replay	10
Input and discussion: Idols and addictions	15
Group exercise: Idol and addiction spotting	20
Sharing together	15
Bible study: Matthew 6.19-33	10
Meditation	10
Putting it into practice	5

Session Three: Remote control

	mins
Welcome and opening prayer	5
Action replay	15
Input and discussion: Remote control	20
Group exercise: Danger – remote control working	15
Bible study: Philemon	20
Meditation	10
Putting it into practice	5

Session Four: The true self and the false self

	mins
Welcome and opening prayer	5
Action replay	15
Input and discussion: The true self and the false self	15
Sharing together	10
Bible study: Luke 3.21-22; Mark 10.46-52; Romans 8.12-17	30
Meditation	10
Putting it into practice	5

Session Five: Global warning

	mins
Welcome and opening prayer	5
Action replay	15
Input and discussion: Global gravity	15
Group exercise: The kingdom among us	20
Bible study: Isaiah 65.17-25	20
Putting it into practice	5
Meditation	10

Sin: Living with gravity

Welcome and opening prayer

If this group has not met before, then fuller introductions will be needed, and time should be taken to do this.

Wherever possible ensure that the welcome and introduction are done by someone who is not the group leader – so as to express the fact that everyone has a contribution to make to the leadership – not just the leader.

The opening prayer should follow.

For an outline and suggestions about the opening prayer, see pages 27–8 above ('The opening prayer').

Input and discussion: What is sin?

The Bible uses many terms to describe sin and evil. Even if we are not sure how to define sin and evil, we know it as a power all too evident in human life.

The following paragraph is also in the members' handout. You may like to refer to it or read it aloud.

After a century of the gulags of Russia, the concentration camps of Germany, the incinerated cities of Hiroshima and Nagasaki in Japan, and the killing fields of Cambodia, Bosnia and Rwanda, it is difficult to see how one can deny that there is something deeply wrong with human nature. Christians call this force evil, and its outworking, sin. But often we have too shallow a view of sin. We think of it too easily in terms of bad behaviour ('sin is whatever would get you into *The News of the World*'). It does result in that, but is has much deeper roots – as modern psychology has discovered in exploring the unconscious motivation.

Sometimes it is good to look at something familiar from another perspective. This session looks at sin as like gravity because:

- *It is an ever-present force.*

- *You can't see it – only its effects.*

- *It is so present that you take it for granted.*

There is another important connection. Like gravity, sin not only pulls us down, it also – as plants so clearly witness – is the means of our growing straight and true.

Ask the group to respond to this in some way: does it make sense to them?

Group exercise: Sin is like …

This section works best if you can get people to work in groups of two or three. In this way several pictures of sin emerge and can be compared at the end. It can be done as one group, but may well provoke less thought and discussion. The idea is for groups to work out their own definition of sin before looking at the Scriptures.

Ask the small groups to reflect on how to complete the sentence: 'Sin is like …'. Encourage them to use their own experience; their knowledge of Scripture; their observation of the world around them. Encourage them as well to make the definitions or the pictures as powerful and as personal as they can.

After discussion, ask them to complete the sentence.

Then ask each small group to give its definition to the others.

Bible study: Romans 1.18-25

At the beginning of Romans, Paul sets out his diagnosis of the human condition we know as sin. It will help you to read the passage through before the meeting and study it carefully, perhaps with a simple commentary. This is not so that you can tell everyone what it is about, but so that you can be prepared to help the group if they get stuck, and have some idea how to answer any questions that arise.

Read the passage together as a whole group.

Sharing together: A redefining moment

Allow some time for silence.

■ *Invite people to share insights from the passage that make them want to change their definition of sin.*

■ *Work together as one group to come up with as comprehensive, but brief, a definition of sin as you can.*

There may well be questions that arise from the study of the passage and you may need to give time to these. However, take care not to get sidetracked from the main subject of the course – and do not allow the group's definition of 'sin' to become a list of 'sins' others commit.

Meditation

See the notes in the introduction for this ('Closing meditation', pp. 28–9). Remember that each session has a new passage to be read aloud, which is in the members' handouts.

Putting it into practice

Agree together to look at life in the coming week from the perspective of sin as the gravity of our situation; with a view to coming back next week to share about occasions when this helped you to understand what was going on, and to know what the right decision was.

Note

For the activity (idol and addiction spotting) next week, you need to start collecting/preparing this a week in advance – so read the notes now, not just before the next meeting!

Summary and example timings

	mins
Welcome and opening prayer	10
Input and discussion: What is sin?	10
Group exercise: Sin is like …	15
Bible study: Romans 1.18-25	25
Sharing together: A redefining moment	10
Meditation	15
Putting it into practice	5

Sin: Living with gravity

Input and discussion: What is sin?

After a century of the gulags of Russia, the concentration camps of Germany, the incinerated cities of Hiroshima and Nagasaki in Japan, and the killing fields of Cambodia, Bosnia and Rwanda, it is difficult to see how one can deny that there is something deeply wrong with human nature. Christians call this force evil, and its outworking, sin.

But often we have too shallow a view of sin. We think of it too easily in terms of bad behaviour ('sin is whatever would get you into *The News of the World*'). It does result in that, but it has much deeper roots – as modern psychology has discovered in exploring our unconscious motivations.

The Bible uses many terms to describe this power. It is all too evident in human life – especially other people!

However, sometimes 'familiarity breeds contempt' and we can benefit from seeing things from a different perspective. One such different way forms the title of this session. Sin is like gravity because:

■ *It is an ever-present force.*

■ *You can't see it – only its effects.*

■ *It is so present that you take it for granted.*

There is another vital connection. Sin, like gravity, not only pulls us down, it also – as plants so clearly witness – is the means of our growing up straight and true. Sin, or rather evil, acts like gravity in that it pulls us down and yet also provokes us to grow up strong and true.

Group exercise: Sin is like …

'Gravity' is not the only way to speak of sin. We can no doubt think of other things that illustrate what it is like. Complete the sentence 'Sin is like …' using, if you can think of one, a verbal picture.

Bible study: Romans 1.18-25

> For the wrath of God is revealed from heaven against all ungodliness and wickedness of those who by their wickedness suppress the truth. For what can be known about God is plain to them, because God has shown it to them. Ever since the creation of the world his eternal power and divine nature, invisible though they are, have been understood and seen through the things he has made. So they are without excuse; for though they knew God, they did not honour him as God or give thanks to him, but they became futile in their thinking, and their senseless minds were darkened. Claiming to be wise, they became fools; and they exchanged the glory of the immortal God for images resembling a mortal human being or birds or four-footed animals or reptiles.

Therefore God gave them up in the lusts of their hearts to impurity, to the degrading of their bodies among themselves, because they exchanged the truth about God for a lie and worshipped and served the creature rather than the Creator, who is blessed for ever! Amen.

Romans 1.18-25

In your groups read this passage from the first chapter of Paul's letter to the Church in Rome. Try and sum up what Paul is saying about sin, in a single word or phrase. It may help to do this by trying to complete the sentence 'Sin is like . . . .'

Sharing together: A redefining moment

Now try to develop one comprehensive definition for the whole group.

Meditation

Lamentation is an important part of Old Testament and Jewish prayer (witness the Wailing Wall in Jerusalem). It is a way of expressing grief to God about the way things are. It is not a way of saying to God how terrible everyone else is, but how terrible we are. Nor is it a wallowing in despair. Rather it is seeing and feeling the brokenness of human life, but allowing that grief to be touched by hope – the hope of peace, of forgiveness and resurrection life, and the coming of the kingdom.

In the meditation there will be a time of silence focusing on a Christian symbol and then one, or both, of these passages may be read out.

> As he came near and saw the city, he wept over it, saying, 'If you, even you, had recognized on this day the things that make for peace! But now they are hidden from your eyes.'
>
> Luke 19.41-42

> Incline your ear, O my God, and hear. Open your eyes and look at our desolation and the city that bears your name. We do not present our supplication before you on the ground of our righteousness, but on the ground of your great mercies. O Lord, hear; O Lord, forgive; O Lord, listen and act and do not delay! For your own sake, O my God, because your city and your people bear your name!
>
> Daniel 9.18-19

After another time of silence, there will be a chance to express our own insights and resolutions in open prayer. Begin your petitions 'Thank you, Lord, for . . .' or 'Lord, help us to . . .'

Putting it into practice

Agree together to look at life in the coming week from the perspective of sin as gravity, or other pictures we have used; with a view to coming back next week to share about occasions when this helped you to understand what was going on, and to know what was the right action to take.

Idols and addictions

You will need a varied selection of current newspapers and magazines for this session. You will also need several sheets of flip chart sized paper and some pots of paper glue for each group. A felt-tip pen for each group will also be needed.

Welcome and opening prayer

For an outline and suggestions about the opening prayer, see pages 27–8 ('The opening prayer').

Action replay

Remind people what we did last week and what we agreed to do. Give a lead to the sharing by starting yourself. Depending on the group, you may want to have a free for all discussion, with each person joining in when they want to – or go round the group one at a time asking each person to contribute and others to respond.

Input and discussion: Idols and addictions

This material is also in the members' handout. You can read it out, ask someone else to read it, or express it in your own words. Try to introduce stories and illustrations that will connect with people – either from your experience or maybe from recent local or national events/personalities. Once you begin to look you will find examples of these three types of addiction all around you.

When we make something or someone the centre of our lives, the ultimate focus for our living, we are making an idol. What we put in God's place may be harmless, or even good in itself – such as generosity, music, church work or animal welfare (to name a few at random). However, by allowing it to take the place of God, it becomes a destructive force within us. We can also make something that is evil in itself, such as greed or racial hatred, an idol too.

One of the deepest motivations for turning something into an idol is the urge to 'get control of life', and give it a focus – of which we are in control. Ironically, by giving ourselves over to something that is less than God, we limit and stunt our own lives. Moreover, when we do so, the idol usually ends up controlling us.

When that happens, our idols become addictions. Once we worship them they torment us. There are three particular forms of addictions.

Substance addictions include obvious things like alcohol and drugs, but we can become addicted to almost anything (e.g. caffeine or chocolate).

Then there are *process addictions*, of which the most obvious are work and shopping. It is not that they are wrong in themselves, it is what some people do with them. Some cases of promiscuous behaviour are about being addicted to sex, or falling in love. It is the process not the person that the addicted 'loves'.

The third kind of addiction is a *relationship addiction*, of which the most obvious (and probably least dangerous) is a teenager's 'idol'. More dangerous is addiction to a controlling person, or the worship of another human being.

The good news is that God has come to set us free from idols and addictions.

During, and at the end of the input, check that group members understand and can identify with what you have talked about. Give space for any questions.

Group exercise: Idol and addiction spotting

For the 'identification parade' you will need plenty of magazines and recent newspapers (especially tabloids), for people to work with. Form groups of three or four people.

Give them: a sheet of flip chart paper, a felt-tip pen and plenty of magazines and newspapers.

Get them, with the help of the magazines and newspapers to:

■ *identify any events, stories, individuals in the public eye, who seem to have idols and/or addictions;*

■ *create a collage of idols and idol-worshippers;*

■ *write any key themes or words on the collage to highlight the idols they have spotted.*

Try to make this a fun event.

Then get each group to share their collage and the idols they have identified.

Sharing together

Get the groups to present their discoveries to each other briefly. As with elsewhere in *Emmaus*, 'presentation' can mean what you want to it to mean. The groups can just report back, or they can produce a short drama, or anything in between. It is up to you and up to the groups. Each situation and each group will be different.

Ask each group to consider each other's picture collage and comment on it. As you lead the discussion, encourage the group to relate what is being said to their own lives and experience. Otherwise idols and addictions will simply become something other people suffer from. You may even want to ask them at the end of the discussion, 'Does anyone have any experience of these things in their own lives or the lives of their family?'

Bible study: Matthew 6.19-33

Read the passage from Matthew. It is printed in the members' handout.

Work out together what Jesus saw as the answers to the questions you have just considered, namely, what are the most likely idols/addictions? Why do they invade human experience? And what is the cure?

What can we do in the setting of a consumer culture to live by a different set of values? What practical steps could we take together and encourage each other in to enable us to say by our lifestyle that, as Christians, we are as dedicated as everyone else to improving our standard of living. But our standard of living is measured by likeness to Jesus.

How could we, as a group, shape our lives in such a way that we live lives that are liberated from the idols and addictions that afflict our particular communities and situations in life?

If people have shared openly about idols and addictions in their own lives, ask the group to think through how those can be overcome.

Meditation

Be aware as you prepare to lead this time of prayer that what has been shared in the session may need to be prayed through with individuals either within or outside the group.

See the notes in the introduction for this ('Closing meditation', pp. 28–9).

Putting it into practice

Encourage people to build on the work of the Bible study in identifying what lifestyle actions we could support one another in, to help us lead a more idol/addiction-free life: for our blessing, for the glory of God and as a sign to people around us. Talk through some of the practical steps the group members might take.

Note

For the activity (remote control working) next week, it is again suggested that you use newspaper reports and magazine cuttings to illustrate the points the group will be working on. You will need to start collecting/preparing for this a week in advance – so, again, read the notes now, not just before the next meeting!

Summary and example timings

	mins
Welcome and opening prayer	5
Action replay	10
Input and discussion: Idols and addictions	15
Group exercise: Idol and addiction spotting	20
Sharing together	15
Bible study: Matthew 6.19-33	10
Meditation	10
Putting it into practice	5

Idols and addictions

Input and discussion: Idols and addictions

When we make something or someone the centre of our lives, the ultimate focus for our living, we are making an idol. What we put in God's place may be harmless, or even good in itself – such as generosity, music, church work or animal welfare (to name a few at random). However, by allowing it to take the place of God, it becomes a destructive force within us. We can also make something that is evil in itself, such as greed or racial hatred, an idol too.

One of the deepest motivations for turning something into an idol is the urge to 'get control of life', and give it a focus – of which we are in control. Ironically, by giving ourselves over to something that is less than God, we limit and stunt our own lives. Moreover, when we do so, the idol usually ends up controlling us.

When that happens, our idols become addictions. Once we worship them they torment us. There are three particular forms of addictions.

Substance addictions include obvious things like alcohol and drugs, but we can become addicted to almost anything (e.g. caffeine or chocolate).

Then there are *process addictions*, of which the most obvious are work and shopping. It is not that they are wrong in themselves, it is what some people do with them. Some cases of promiscuous behaviour are about being addicted to sex, or falling in love. It is the process not the person that the addicted 'loves'.

The third kind of addiction is a *relationship addiction*, of which the most obvious (and probably least dangerous) is a teenager's 'idol'. More dangerous is addiction to a controlling person, or the worship of another human being.

The good news is that God has come to set us free from idols and addictions.

How do you respond to this?

Bible study: Matthew 6.19-33

Do not store up for yourselves treasures on earth, where moth and rust consume and where thieves break in and steal; but store up for yourselves treasures in heaven, where neither moth nor rust consumes and where thieves
do not break in and steal. For where your treasure is, there your heart will be also.

The eye is the lamp of the body. So, if your eye is healthy, your whole body will be full of light; but if your eye is unhealthy, your whole body will be full of darkness. If then the light in you is darkness, how great is the darkness!

No one can serve two masters; for a slave will either hate the one and love the other, or be devoted to the one and despise the other. You cannot serve God and wealth. Therefore I tell you, do not worry about your life, what you will eat or what you will drink, or about your body, what you will wear. Is not life more than food, and the body more than clothing? Look at the birds of the air; they neither sow nor reap nor gather into barns, and yet your heavenly Father feeds them. Are you not of more value than they? And can any of you by worrying add a single hour to your span of life? And why do you worry about clothing? Consider the lilies of the field, how they grow; they neither toil nor spin, yet I tell you, even Solomon in all his glory was not clothed like one of these. But if God so clothes the grass of the field, which is alive today and tomorrow is thrown into the oven, will he not much more clothe you – you of little faith? Therefore do not worry, saying, 'What will we eat?' or 'What will we drink?' or 'What will we wear?' For it is the Gentiles who strive for all these things; and indeed your heavenly Father knows that you need all these things. But strive first for the kingdom of God and his righteousness, and all these things will be given to you as well.

Matthew 6.19-33

Work out together what Jesus saw as the answers to the questions you have just considered, namely:

- *What are the most likely idols and addictions?*

- *Why do they invade human experience?*

- *What is the cure?*

- *What can we do in the setting of a consumer culture to live by a different set of values?*

- *What practical steps could we take and encourage each other in together to enable us to say by our lifestyle that, as Christians, we are as dedicated as everyone else to improving our standard of living. But our standard of living is measured by likeness to Jesus.*

- *How could we, as a group, shape our lives in such a way that we live lives that are liberated from the idols and addictions which afflict our particular communities and situations in life?*

> The purpose of the Church is to manifest an alternative way of seeing and living life.
>
> John Westerhoff, *Living the Faith Community*

Meditation

In the meditation there will be a time of silence focusing on a Christian symbol and then the following quotation will be said as a focus for our meditation, and to help us identify anything that has the wrong place in our lives.

> My god is that which
> rivets my attention
> centres my activity
> preoccupies my mind
> and motivates my action.
>
> Luke Johnson, *Sharing Possessions*

Remote control

You will need to prepare in advance either some pictures from newspapers and magazines or some short video clips for this session. See the notes in the section on the group exercise.

Welcome and opening prayer

For an outline and suggestions about the opening prayer see pages 27–8 ('The opening prayer').

Action replay

Remind people of what we did last week and what we agreed to do. Give a lead to the sharing by starting yourself.

As the sharing takes place, avoid any sense of giving superficial answers. Often Christians have to struggle to overcome destructive patterns of behaviour over many months rather than a few days. It may be that the group needs to suggest, lovingly, ongoing ways to overcome idols and addictions in members' lives – or needs to agree to hold one another accountable over the longer term about these things.

Input and discussion: Remote control

(It may help you as you go through the notes to have an actual remote control for a TV or audio system as a visual aid.)

In the last session we looked at idols and addictions. They relate particularly to how we abuse God's creation as the gravity of sin distorts and 'pulls down' our response to grace and life. This is not entirely a matter of how we handle things – people get sucked into our idols and addictions too – but the emphasis tends to be on the abuse of things.

In this session we turn our attention to the impact of the gravity of sin on relationships. The two key ideas we shall consider are *remote* and *control*.

Remote control

When archaeologists of the future come to dig up the remains of some long-lost twenty-first-century settlement, they will probably conclude that the remote control gadget for our televisions was the key tool we used.

Certainly, so much in life is about control. Control of the environment, control in politics and controlling other people. We easily want to dictate how people act and even think. The world has shown us, from Hitler to Stalin, and through many others, how addicted we are to having control over people. But Jesus came, modelling a new way. He spoke with authority, yet he never sought to control others; rather he came to 'save', to set people free. Jesus has shown us a life ordered around the power of love, rather than the love of power. Our goals with other people, too, need to be about setting them free, giving them space, liberating them.

Our society has so emphasized the individual, individualism and 'doing your own thing' that we are clearly hungering for a sense of belonging: for love and for intimacy. Yet we are not good at relationships. We keep our distance; and stay remote. We either invade other people's space (that is what domineering behaviour, and physical, emotional and sexual abuse are all about), or we become cut off, isolated, lonely and longing for a sense of belonging.

Some of this material is also in the members' handout. You can either read it out, ask someone else to read or express it in your own words, introducing stories and illustrations that will easily connect with people's experience. You may want to draw on recent local or national events and personalities.

Encourage some group discussion. Does this make sense? Are there ways in which members of the group have seen the urge to be remote, and in control, evident in the world?

Are there areas of our own lives where we are aware of these urges?

Group exercise: Danger – remote control working

You will need to have prepared this in advance.

Either

Collect from newspapers and magazines different illustrations of 'remoteness' and inappropriate 'control'. Split the group into pairs, giving each pair a picture. Invite them to describe to each other what they see going on. Pass the pictures on and repeat the exercise.

Or

Prepare up to five short video clips from the television: soap operas; commercials; drama series; children's cartoons or films. Comedy often turns on remoteness or control and a clip from *Fawlty Towers* or *Mr Bean* would lighten up what could otherwise be a difficult subject. Show the clips one at a time to the whole group and ask them to comment on what they see happening. Don't forget to use your remote control as you show them.

At the end of the exercise again ask the group whether they identify with any of this in their own lives, their work situation or the life of their family.

Bible study: Philemon

Read the whole of the letter of Paul to Philemon. It is very nearly the shortest book in the Bible, but it is still quite a large passage to read out all at once. If members of the group are happy about reading aloud, split the reading between different voices.

Before you read the letter, it may help to set briefly the context and reason it was written. It's fairly easy to work out from the text but a short commentary may help you here.

As a group ask the following questions. The idea is to make a connection between this story and our experience today.

■   *How does our experience of life get near to this sort of experience?*

■   *What can we learn from the way that Paul handles a difficult social conflict?*

■   *What could we practise in the coming week, in the light of these reflections?*

It might be best to explore these questions in pairs before addressing them as a whole group.

Wherever possible, relate the questions and the answers to the actual situations people have described.

Meditation

See the notes in the introduction for this ('Closing meditation', pp. 28–9). Remember that each session has a new passage to be read aloud, which is in the members' handouts.

Putting it into practice

Some of this discussion will, we hope, have already taken place during the Bible study.

- *What actions do we sense God calling us to take to live in the freedom and intimacy he has won for us?*

- *How can we give that intimacy and space to others this week?*

- *How do we stop using our remote control?*

Summary and example timings

	mins
Welcome and opening prayer	5
Action replay	15
Input and discussion: Remote control	20
Group exercise: Danger – remote control working	15
Bible study: Philemon	20
Meditation	10
Putting it into practice	5

Remote control

Input and discussion: Remote control

When archaeologists of the future come to dig up the remains of some long-lost twenty-first-century settlement, they will probably conclude that the remote control we use for our televisions was the key tool we used.

Our culture wants to stay *remote*, keeping our space and protecting our freedom. But we are also very committed to being in *control*. Control of the environment, control in politics and controlling other people. We easily want to dictate how people act and even think. The world has shown us, from Hitler to Stalin, and through many others, how addicted we are to having control over people. But Jesus came, modelling a new way. He spoke with authority, yet he never sought to control others; rather he came to 'save', to set people free. Jesus has shown us a life ordered around the power of love, rather than the love of power. Our goals with other people, too, need to be about setting them free, giving them space, liberating them.

Bible study: Philemon

Paul, a prisoner of Christ Jesus, and Timothy our brother,
To Philemon our dear friend and co-worker, to Apphia our sister, to Archippus our fellow-soldier, and to the church in your house:
Grace to you and peace from God our Father and the Lord Jesus Christ.

When I remember you in my prayers, I always thank my God because I hear of your love for all the saints and your faith towards the Lord Jesus. I pray that the sharing of your faith may become effective when you perceive all the good that we may do for Christ. I have indeed received much joy and encouragement from your love, because the hearts of the saints have been refreshed through you, my brother.

For this reason, though I am bold enough in Christ to command you to do your duty, yet I would rather appeal to you on the basis of love – and I, Paul, do this as an old man, and now also as a prisoner of Christ Jesus. I am appealing to you for my child, Onesimus, whose father I have become during my imprisonment. Formerly he was useless to you, but now he is indeed useful both to you and to me. I am sending him, that is, my own heart, back to you. I wanted to keep him with me, so that he might be of service to me in your place during my imprisonment for the gospel; but I preferred to do nothing without your consent, in order that your good deed might be voluntary and not something forced. Perhaps this is the reason he was separated from you for a while, so that you might have him back forever, no longer as a slave but more than a slave, a beloved brother – especially to me but how much more to you, both in the flesh and in the Lord.

So if you consider me your partner, welcome him as you would welcome me. If he has wronged you in any way, or owes you anything, charge that to my account. I, Paul, am writing this with my own hand: I will repay it. I say nothing about your owing me even your own self. Yes, brother, let me have this benefit from you in the Lord! Refresh my heart in Christ. Confident of your obedience, I am writing to you, knowing that you will do even more than I say.

One thing more – prepare a guest room for me, for I am hoping through your prayers to be restored to you.

Epaphras, my fellow prisoner in Christ Jesus, sends greetings to you, and so do Mark, Aristarchus, Demas, and Luke, my fellow workers.

The grace of the Lord Jesus Christ be with your spirit.

Philemon 1-25

Read the whole of Paul's letter to Philemon. Consider it in the light of what we have considered already about being remote, and being in control.

Identify where Paul gives people space, how he seeks to motivate people to right actions, and what sort of example he himself sets.

Ask one another the following questions:

- *How does our experience of life get near to this sort of experience?*

- *What can we learn from the way that Paul handles a difficult social conflict?*

- *What could we practise in the coming week, in the light of these reflections?*

Meditation

In the meditation there will be a time of silence focusing on a Christian symbol. Then these words of Jesus may form the main focus for our meditation.

Jesus said:

> The thief comes only to steal and kill and destroy. I came that they may have life, and have it abundantly.
>
> John 10.10

> We renounce every attempt to rob us of life by our being controlled by others, or by our being kept remote from them.
> We repent of ways that we keep remote, or seek control.
> We rejoice in God's desire to be close, yet set us free.
> We resolve to act that way in our relationships with others.

Putting it into practice

Use the fruits of the meditation and our discussions in the Bible study to plan what actions we sense God is calling us to take to live in the freedom and intimacy he has won for us, and to give that intimacy and space to others this week.

The true self and the false self

Welcome and opening prayer

For an outline and suggestions about the opening prayer see pages 27–8
('The opening prayer').

Action replay

Remind people of what we did last week and what we agreed to do.
Give a lead to the sharing by starting yourself.

In particular we went through a series of steps of renouncing every attempt to
rob us of life by our being controlled by others, of repenting of ways that we keep remote,
or seek to control others. We rejoiced in God's desire to be close to us, yet set us free. We
resolved to act that way in our relationships with others. We then used that meditation to
shape our plans for how to live in freedom from sin and in intimacy with God.

Now we report back about how we got on; what we learned or found ourselves struggling
with; and how we intend to go on putting this into practice.

Input and discussion: The true self and the false self

The story so far . . .

In the first three sessions we considered the nature of sin.

1   Sin is like gravity. It is a force that pulls us down, and yet – in the purposes of God –
     is that which provokes us to grow up.

2   The gravity of sin pulls us down into idols and addictions that distort our lives.

3   This leads us either to keep our distance from others (being *remote*), and/or to get
     power over them (being in *control*) – and other people often do the same to us.

In these last two sessions we look at how this distorting effect (the 'gravity') of sin affects:

■   *our own lives and identity – (our subject for this session);*

■   *the whole of human society and the whole life of the globe.*

The impact of sin on our personal lives

The Bible points to a division within all of us – between the false self, which organizes life as
though it, or some idol/addiction, were God, and the true self, which emerges when we live life
before God.

The false self sees itself as the centre of life. The true self moves beyond self-awareness to being
alive to life, others and God – it can transcend ('go beyond') itself.

The false self tries to hide, achieve, please and control. The true self is able to flow between
giving and receiving, commanding and being directed, as the situation requires.

The false self finds its focus in itself and its own actions, the true self reaches out to listen to God and to act in obedience to that which it hears.

The false self is 'turned in on' the self. The true self is open to God and life. God, by the Spirit, addresses the true self that is called into life by Christ.

This is what Scripture means when it teaches that we are both 'in Adam' and also 'in Christ' (see Romans 5.12-21 and Romans 6.1-14) and that there is a battle within (Romans 8.1-17).

(There is no need to read these passages out. One of them is going to be looked at in some detail later on. However, it will help you as leader to read them and think about them before the session begins.)

This point is also evident in other writings of Paul (notably Galatians 2.20, Ephesians 4.20-24 and Colossians 3.5-14 where the images of 'putting to death' and 'putting on' are used). The old self listens to inner, and outer, negative ideas, demands and expectations; the new self listens to God and responds positively to the challenges that life brings.

This is expressed well by Leanne Payne:

> As a result of the Fall, mankind slipped from God-consciousness into the hell of self and self-consciousness. This fallen self, turned inward . . . dwells in misconceived feelings and attitudes, those that arise from listening to the self-in-separation and to the voices of a fallen world.
>
> A right understanding of the true self and our acceptance of it is necessary . . . In accepting myself in Him, I am no longer trapped in the mode of trying to win my righteousness or God's love. We are becoming persons. We become as we remain in Christ. Focused on the word the Father is always sending, obedient to it, the new self is not in bondage to the voices the old self listened to.
>
> Leanne Payne, *The Healing Presence*, pp. 47–8

Paul writes:

> So if anyone is in Christ, there is a new creation: everything old has passed away; see, everything has become new!
>
> 2 Corinthians 5.17

This quotation and all of these notes are on the members' handouts.

After the input ask the group whether this makes sense to them. (Probably some of it will not at a first hearing – give people permission to say this.) This is one of the harder ideas to communicate in the course. You may need to go back over the points a couple of times until most of the group have grasped the essence of what you are trying to say.

Sharing together

In pairs discuss and share with one another occasions when we have been true to ourselves and false to ourselves.

You may need to give some examples from your own experience to give people some idea of what you mean.

Bible study: Luke 3.21-22; Mark 10.46-52; Romans 8.12-17

The three passages we are looking at are printed in the members' handout. If people were involved in the group when it did the previous module ('Living images') then they will have studied this before. The value of using it, briefly, is to remind and reinforce the study from that session.

First take people through Luke 3.21-22.

Note how Jesus experiences:

- *being loved (the words of the voice and the action of the dove);*

- *being addressed (the Father calls him into his identity as the Son);*

- *being sent: this is the 'word from heaven'.*

Part of this comes from Psalm 2.7, about David's kingdom, and part from Isaiah 42.1, about the suffering servant. He is sent to model a life of servant authority – renouncing the love of power, he embraces the power of love.

This is the core shape of our new nature – we are loved, addressed and sent.

Then split the group in two. Ask them to see how this core shape of our new nature works out for:

- *Bartimaeus – read Mark 10.46-52. How is he loved, addressed and sent?*

- *The new creation/person in Christ – read Romans 8.12-17. How are we, the children of God, loved, addressed and sent?*

Ask the groups to work out together how this should affect our attitude to ourselves. Do we believe the 'old self' or the 'new self'?

Make sure there is time for the groups to report back to each other.

As part of the reporting back, apply what has been learned from the Bible study to the things about themselves that people shared earlier in the session.

Meditation

See the notes in the introduction for this ('Closing meditation', pp. 28–9). Remember that each session has a new passage to be read aloud, which is in the members' handouts.

Putting it into practice

What might God want us to 'put off' or 'put on'?

How shall we live out the truths we have been exploring?

It will be wise at this point in the course to remind everyone that this is the most important part of the study: agreeing how we put things into action, doing it and then being in some way accountable to one another.

Summary and example timings

	mins
Welcome and opening prayer	5
Action replay	15
Input and discussion: The true self and the false self	15
Sharing together	10
Bible study: Luke 3.21-22; Mark 10.46-52; Romans 8.12-17	30
Meditation	10
Putting it into practice	5

The true self and the false self

Input and discussion: The true self and the false self

In the first three sessions we considered the nature of sin.

■ *First we considered sin as being like gravity, the force that pulls us down, and yet – in the purposes of God – that which provokes us to grow up.*

■ *We then looked at ways in which the gravity of sin pulls us down in idols and addictions that distort our lives.*

■ *In the last session we thought about how we try either to keep our distance from others (being remote), and/or to get power over them (being in control) – and how they often do the same to us.*

The impact of sin on our personal lives

Sin has a great impact on our personal lives. The Bible points to a division within all of us – between the false self, which organizes life as though it, or some idol/addiction, were God, and the true self, which emerges when we live life before God.

The false self sees itself as the centre of life, the true self moves beyond self-awareness to being alive to life, others and God – it can transcend ('go beyond') itself. The false self tries to hide, achieve, please and control. The true self is able to flow between giving and receiving, commanding and being directed, as the situation requires.

The false self finds its focus in itself and its own actions, the true self reaches out to listen to God and to act in obedience to that which it hears.

The false self is 'turned in on the self'. The true self is open to God and life. God, by the Spirit, addresses the true self that is called into life by Christ.

This is what Scripture means when it teaches that we are both 'in Adam' (the false self) and also 'in Christ' (the true self). You can read about this in Paul's letter to the Romans, especially 5.12-21 and 6.1-14, and about the battle within (Romans 8.1-17).

This point is also evident in other writings of Paul (notably Galatians 2.20, Ephesians 4.20-24 and Colossians 3.5-14 where the images of 'putting to death' and 'putting on' are used). The old self listens to inner, and outer, negative ideas, demands and expectations; the new self listens to God and responds positively to the challenges that life brings.

This is expressed well by Leanne Payne:

> As a result of the Fall, mankind slipped from God-consciousness into the hell of self and self-consciousness. This fallen self, turned inward . . . dwells in misconceived feelings and attitudes, those that arise from listening to the self-in-separation and to the voices of a fallen world.

A right understanding of the true self and our acceptance of it is necessary ... In accepting myself in Him, I am no longer trapped in the mode of trying to win my righteousness or God's love. We are becoming persons. We become as we remain in Christ. Focused on the word the Father is always sending, obedient to it, the new self is not in bondage to the voices the old self listened to.

Leanne Payne, *The Healing Presence*, pp. 47–8

Paul writes:

So if anyone is in Christ, there is a new creation: everything old has passed away; see, everything has become new!

2 Corinthians 5.17

Sharing together

In pairs discuss and share with one another occasions when we have been true to ourselves and false to ourselves.

Bible study

We are going to look at three passages.

I   Luke 3.21-22: Jesus is baptized

Now when all the people were baptized, and when Jesus also had been baptized and was praying, the heaven was opened, and the Holy Spirit descended upon him in bodily form like a dove. And a voice came from heaven, 'You are my Son, the Beloved; with you I am well pleased.'

Luke 3.21-22

Note how Jesus experiences:

- *being loved (the words of the voice and the action of the dove);*

- *being addressed (the Father calls him into his identity as the Son);*

- *being sent: this is the 'word from heaven'.*

Part of this comes from Psalm 2.7, about David's kingdom, and part from Isaiah 42.1, about the suffering servant. He is sent to model a life of servant authority – renouncing the love of power, he embraces the power of love. This is the core shape of our new nature – we are loved, addressed and sent.

Share stories of times when we have experienced being loved, addressed, and/or sent.

2   Mark 10.46-52: Blind Bartimaeus

They came to Jericho. As he and his disciples and a large crowd were leaving Jericho, Bartimaeus son of Timaeus, a blind beggar, was sitting by the roadside. When he heard that it was Jesus of Nazareth, he began to shout out and say, 'Jesus, Son of David, have mercy on me!' Many sternly ordered him to be quiet, but he cried out even more loudly, 'Son of David, have mercy on me!' Jesus stood still and said, 'Call him here.' And they called the blind man, saying to him, 'Take heart; get up, he is calling you.' So, throwing off his cloak, he sprang up and came to Jesus. Then Jesus said to him, 'What do you want me to do for you?' The blind man said to him, 'My teacher, let me see again.' Jesus said to him, 'Go; your faith has made you well.' Immediately he regained his sight and followed him on the way.

How does Bartimaeus experience being loved, addressed and sent?

Mark 10.46-52

3   Romans 8.12-17: The children of God

So then, brothers and sisters, we are debtors, not to the flesh, to live according to the flesh – for if you live according to the flesh, you will die; but if by the Spirit you put to death the deeds of the body, you will live. For all who are led by the Spirit of God are children of God. For you did not receive a spirit of slavery to fall back into fear; but you have received a spirit of adoption. When we cry, 'Abba! Father!' it is that very Spirit bearing witness with our spirit that we are children of God, and if children, then heirs, heirs of God and joint heirs with Christ – if, in fact, we suffer with him so that we may also be glorified with him.

Romans 8.12-17

In what ways are we, as the children of God, loved, addressed and sent?

We should also work out how this should affect our attitude to ourselves. Do we believe the 'old self' or the 'new self'?

Meditation

A Scripture to ponder:

You were taught to put away your former way of life, your old self, corrupt and deluded by its lusts, and to be renewed in the spirit of your minds, and to clothe yourselves with the new self, created according to the likeness of God in true righteousness and holiness.

Ephesians 4.22-24

Take time to consider what attitudes belong to the old self and what to the new self in our own lives.

Putting it into practice

How can we live as people who are loved, addressed and sent by God?

What might God want us/me to 'put off' or 'put on'?

Remember, this is the most important part of the study: agreeing how to live with our lives the gospel we proclaim with our lips. As Jesus put it: 'blessed . . . are those who hear the word of God and obey it' (Luke 11.28).

Global warning

Welcome and opening prayer

For an outline and suggestions about the opening prayer, see pages 27–8 ('The opening prayer') above.

Action replay

Remind people of what we did in the last session and what we agreed to do. Give a lead to the sharing by starting yourself.

Input and discussion: Global gravity

This final session considers the effect of evil on the world around us. The same inner battle that we experience between our true self and our false self goes on in human relations – in social organizations (such as schools, workplace, industry, governments and – yes – churches), and in the environment too.

There are three phases of global gravity to look at.

1   The reality of evil in human society

The Scriptures are full of stories that witness to this reality of evil.

The story of the Fall involves not just a break in relation with God, but the first marital problem, a struggle with creativity (work and childbirth), and environmental problems (thorns and briars).

The Tower of Babel illustrates the destructive effects of an over-developed 'drive for power'.

Wars, floods, plagues fill the pages of the Bible: all is not well with planet earth.

2   The hope of a new order

The opening books of the Bible introduce us to three great themes of hope:

Sabbath (rest), Jubilee (liberation), Shalom (peace/wholeness).

The prophets spoke of a new day, a new order and a new covenant.

Jesus came proclaiming the good news of the kingdom – God's rule breaking in.

3   The signs of victory over evil that are already present

Hebrews 11 catalogues the men and women of faith who lived in the present by the values and truth of the world to come, of whom Jesus is the supreme example (Hebrews 12).

We are to look for the kingdom as already present and to pray for its coming (Lord's Prayer). Pentecost reverses Babel – here and now.

This is a lot to present in a short time! It may be best to choose one example from each of the three sections. The important things to get over are that:

■   *evil is a reality in our society and not just in us;*

- *the Christian faith has always looked for a new order of rest, liberation and peace;*

- *in Christ we see that the victory has already been won and what we used to think of as belonging only to the future breaks into our present.*

Group exercise: The kingdom among us

Split the group up and ask them to identify ways, in history and in the present, here and in other parts of the world, where they can see signs of God's new order breaking in. It will be helpful if they can be given large sheets of paper and marker pens for this.

For instance:

- *Where are there situations of hope in the world?*

- *Where are Sabbath (rest), Jubilee (liberation) and Shalom (peace) evident?*

- *Where (in relationships, businesses, communities, organizations, nations) are there signs of victory over the gravity of evil?*

- *Where can we see people working to reverse the tide of destructive forces?*

The purpose of this list is to remind us that the kingdom is among us.

Encourage people to speak about their own experiences as well as the big examples of national and political life.

There may well be people in the group with particular ecological concerns. It is important to draw these out. The ecological crisis is one of the great issues of our age.

Bible study: Isaiah 65.17-25

The vision is on a cosmic scale, yet the issues are the ones that many communities face:

- *the longing for, and lack of real community (vv. 18-19);*

- *infant mortality (v. 20);*

- *the needs of the elderly (v. 20);*

- *poverty, housing and employment (vv. 21-24);*

- *in and through it all, a spiritual hunger (v. 24);*

- *and environmental issues have their place too (v. 25).*

It looks like a very contemporary vision.

In what ways are any of us involved with these issues?

How can we be, in all of life, part of God's solution, rather than part of the world's problem? (Though in the affluent West we cannot escape being part of the problem too.)

Get people to give examples of things with which they are already involved.

Discuss what you could be doing:

- *as individuals;*

- *as a group;*

- *as a church.*

Putting it into practice

Invite people to consider what they have learned in this session and throughout the whole course.

How has it changed their attitude or behaviour? Have a few minutes' discussion and then ask everyone to write down one or two things that stand out for them as things they have learned and as resolutions they wish to make. These can be used in the meditation that follows.

Meditation

See the notes in the introduction for this ('Closing meditation', pp. 28–9).

There is no specific passage for this session.

Get people to look at the things they have written down. If they wish to they could read these aloud, or else just pray them quietly in their hearts.

Some of the things we have learnt will make us want to weep and lament for the brokenness of our world.

The resolutions we have made will enable us to join our voices in rejoicing for the good news of the coming kingdom. We are to be part of that good news by our actions.

Summary and example timings

	mins
Welcome and opening prayer	5
Action replay	15
Input and discussion: Global gravity	15
Group exercise: The kingdom among us	20
Bible study: Isaiah 65.17-25	20
Putting it into practice	5
Meditation	10

Global warning

Input and discussion: Global gravity

This final session considers the effect of evil on the world around us. The same inner battle that we experience between our true self and our false self goes on in human relations – in social organizations (such as schools, workplace, industry, governments, yes – and churches), and in the environment too.

There are three phases of global gravity to look at:

1   The reality of evil in human society

The Scriptures are full of stories that witness to this reality. In the book of Genesis we read about the fall of humanity. We are imprisoned by our wrong choices. The story of the Tower of Babel (Genesis 11.1-9) is all about the destructive effects of an over-developed drive for power. Wars, floods, plagues fill its pages: all is not well with planet earth.

2   The hope of a new order

The opening books of the Bible introduce us to three great themes of hope: Sabbath (rest), Jubilee (liberation), Shalom (peace/wholeness).

The prophets spoke of a new day, a new order and a new covenant. Jesus comes proclaiming the good news of the kingdom – God's rule breaking in.

3   The signs of victory over evil that are already present

Hebrews 11 catalogues the men and women of faith who lived in the present by the values and truth of the world to come, of whom Jesus is the supreme example (Hebrews 12).

We are to look for the kingdom as already present and to pray for its coming (Lord's Prayer). Pentecost reverses Babel – here and now.

All this tells us that:

■   *evil is a reality in our society and not just in us;*

■   *the Christian faith has always looked for a new order of rest, liberation and peace;*

■   *in Christ we see that the victory has already been won and what we used to think of as belonging only to the future breaks into our present.*

Group exercise: The kingdom among us

Identify ways, in history and in the present, here and in other parts of the world, where you can see signs of God's new order breaking in.

■   *Where is hope being given?*

■   *Where are Sabbath (rest), Jubilee (liberation) and Shalom (peace) evident?*

■   *Where (in relationships, businesses, communities, organizations, nations) are there signs of victory over the gravity of evil?*

■   *Where can we see people working to reverse the tide of destructive forces?*

Make the list as wide ranging as possible. It is to remind us that the kingdom is among us.

One of the great issues of our day is the ecological crisis facing our planet. Sometimes Christian think of themselves as so distinct from the rest of creation as to be separate from it. Modern urban life is alienated from natural relations with the creation. It is this which has led to the exploitation of creation. We have lost our sense of a creator God.

This exploitative understanding of dominion over the creation is part of the evil in our modern world and needs to be balanced with a hope for a new order in which we recover our understanding of ourselves as creatures who are part of the creation. Dominion in the biblical sense is about stewardship, not power.

We distort the Christian message if we separate God as saviour from God as creator.

People will want to listen to a Church that takes seriously the ecological questions of our day.

Bible study: Isaiah 65.17-25

For I am about to create new heavens
and a new earth;
the former things shall not be remembered
or come to mind.
But be glad and rejoice forever
in what I am creating;
for I am about to create Jerusalem as a joy,
and its people as a delight.
I will rejoice in Jerusalem,
and delight in my people;
no more shall the sound of weeping be heard in it,
or the cry of distress.
No more shall there be in it
an infant that lives but a few days,
or an old person who does not live out a lifetime;
for one who dies at a hundred years will be considered a youth,
and one who falls short of a hundred will be considered accursed.
They shall build houses and inhabit them;
they shall plant vineyards and eat their fruit.
They shall not build and another inhabit;
they shall not plant and another eat;
for like the days of a tree shall the days of my people be,
and my chosen shall long enjoy the work of their hands.
They shall not labour in vain,
or bear children for calamity;
for they shall be offspring blessed by the Lord –
and their descendants as well.
Before they call I will answer,
while they are yet speaking I will hear.
The wolf and the lamb shall feed together,
the lion shall eat straw like the ox;
but the serpent – its food shall be dust!
They shall not hurt or destroy
on all my holy mountain,
says the Lord.

Isaiah 65.17-25

This vision of Isaiah's is on a cosmic scale, yet the issues are the ones that many communities face:

- *the longing for, and lack of real community (vv. 18-19);*

- *infant mortality (v. 20);*

- *the needs of the elderly (v. 20);*

- *poverty, housing and employment (vv. 21-24);*

- *in and through it all, a spiritual hunger (v. 24);*

- *and environmental issues have their place too (v. 25).*

It looks like a very contemporary vision.

In what ways are any of us involved with these issues?

How can we be, in all of life, part of God's solution, rather than part of the world's problem? (Though in the affluent West we cannot escape being part of the problem too.)

Discuss what we could be doing

- *as individuals;*

- *as a group;*

- *as a church.*

Personal identity

Introduction

The aim of this *Emmaus* course is to give people an awareness of:

■   *their new identity in Christ;*

■   *the spiritual battle involved in living in that new identity;*

■   *the grace that enables us to love God and others because we are accepted.*

Session 1: The search for identity

Understanding the roots of the modern search for identity and how we can be in touch with our own sense of identity.

Session 2: The gift of identity

Seeing the nature of the new identity that Christ gives the believer and seeing how to receive and live in these gifts.

Session 3: The model of identity

Considering Jesus and how he lived out of a positive identity and how that applies to our own sense of self-acceptance.

Session 4: The battle for identity

Recognizing the battle between the old self and the new creation and discovering how to participate in the death of the old, and the growth of the new, nature.

Session 5: Living beyond the search for identity

Living out the two great commandments takes us more effectively into the new identity than an endless introspective search.

In leading this session, avoid a teacher/pupil, provider/client approach, and seek at all times to empower others. 'You can do it' is much to be preferred to 'let me tell you'.

Some groups are 'dead, flat, formal' and change nothing and nobody. Other groups are life-changing experiences. Two keys to experiencing the latter are the leaders' openness, honesty and modelling of vulnerability; and a 'critical mass of expectation of encountering God'. Some form of prayer support/backup is likely to prove decisive.

Following the pattern of the other courses in this part of *Emmaus*, we suggest that a different member of the group leads the welcome and opening prayer for each session. You may also want to share out other tasks in the life of the group during this course.

Some of the material in this *Emmaus* course may be unfamiliar to you as a leader or to the members of your group. For this reason, we have provided two members' handouts for each session. The main handout contains a summary of the main points of the input and the group exercises, as with the other units.

The second handout is a short essay on the theme of identity. You may want to copy this handout for the group and give it out either before or after the session for background reading or further reading. You may want to read out parts of it during the session – or simply use it for your own background reading and preparation.

There is meditation in each session. This works best if the structure and much of the content are the same each week.

No music/worship songs are proposed. They are best added according to the tradition of your own church or group.

As with the other *Emmaus* courses, some background reading by the leaders, though not essential, would be helpful. In order of priority, you may like to have a look at:

Henri Nouwen, *Life of the Beloved*, Hodder and Stoughton, 1992.

Leanne Payne, *The Healing Presence*, Kingsway, 1989.

Session One: The search for identity

	mins
Welcome and opening prayer	5
Group exercise: Significant things	10
Input and discussion: The search for identity	15
Bible study and discussion: What's in a name?	15
Bible study and discussion: A new name	10
Group exercise: How do you see yourself?	20
Prayer together	10
Putting it into practice	5

Session Two: The gift of identity

	mins
Welcome and opening prayer	5
Reporting back	10
Input and discussion: Finding my identity in Christ	20
Bible study and discussion: The new self	20
Group exercise: Becoming a new person	20
Meditation	10
Putting it into practice	5

Session Three: The model of identity

	mins
Welcome and opening prayer	5
Reporting back	10
Input and discussion: Looking at Jesus	20
Bible study and discussion: Jesus, you and me	20
Group exercise: Describing ourselves	20
Meditation	10
Putting it into practice	5

Session Four: The battle for identity

	mins
Welcome and opening prayer	5
Reporting back	10
Input and discussion: Understanding the battle	20
Bible study and discussion: The battle within	15
Group exercise: Describing our journey	20
Meditation	10
Putting it into practice	10

Session Five: Living beyond the search for identity

	mins
Welcome and opening prayer	5
Reporting back	10
Input and discussion: Freedom from self-concern	20
Bible study and discussion: From the old to the new	20
Group exercise: Looking back and looking forward	20
Prayer together	10

The search for identity

Welcome and opening prayer

At the start of this module take time to introduce yourselves to each other. Then one of the group should open in prayer, asking God to be present as the group explores together the theme of identity.

Group exercise: Significant things

Give everyone a piece of paper and pencil. Get them to fold the paper into four.

- *In the top left-hand square identify one of the happiest moments of your childhood.*

- *In the top right-hand square identify your favourite meal.*

- *In the bottom left-hand square name the person (dead or alive) you most admire.*

- *In the bottom right-hand square write the name you would like if you could not use your present one.*

Either as a whole group, or in pairs/triplets, share together what you have written.

Input and discussion: The search for identity

Go through the points on the main members' handout, bringing in other questions and insights on the optional handout for this session (see pp. 68–9).

Identity is knowing who I am. Many people today are uncertain who they are and are not at peace with themselves.

Values and ideals that used to give people identity in our society are changing all the time. Where should we look to find out who we are?

Some influences today (mainly from the East) are saying: 'lose your identity in the greater universe'. Others (from the New Age movement) say: 'look inside yourself more'.

As Christians we believe we find our true identity in who we are in God's sight.

Bible study and discussion: What's in a name?

Give a brief introduction to the importance of names and naming in the Bible.

Allow people to share their own stories about naming then read Genesis 2.19-24 (on the members' handout).

Talk together about our good and bad, sad and funny experiences of naming, with a view to exploring as many aspects of naming as possible. Try to answer these questions together:

- *Why didn't God tell Adam the names of the animals?*

- *Why is naming things important?*

- *Does anyone have a story about when a doctor named their condition? Or a story of the problems of not knowing the names of things or people?*

- *What happens when we get names wrong? Does anyone have a story of wrong diagnosis (by doctor or car mechanic, etc.)?*

- *What happens when names are used destructively? (Playground memories?)*

Bible study and discussion: A new name

Read Matthew 16.13-20 (text is on members' handout). Explore the impact of Peter's new name, noting:

- *How others in Scripture received a new name as a result of an encounter with God (Abram to Abraham, Saul to Paul).*

- *How Peter became ('grew into') his new name, especially through the impact of the day of Pentecost.*

- *How his identity seemed to be continually developing.*

Group exercise: How do you see yourself?

Ask each person to fold another piece of paper in four, put the letter 'F' (for 'female') in the top left-hand corner of the top square, and the letter 'M' ('male') in the top right-hand corner. Put the names of the most significant influences on you in your growing years (birth to 16). (Not always parents.)

- *In the top two squares (below the names) list ways in which you see yourself as being like those you have identified.*

- *In the bottom two squares note the ways in which you see yourself as different from them.*

- *In the same pairs/triplets, share what this tells you about how you see yourself.*

Prayer together

Subdue the lighting (table lamps or candles, not top lights), and invite people to sit comfortably and relax. Slow down the pace of the meeting and your talking.

Put a candle in the centre of the room (on a table) and light it. Use this sentence as a response:

Leader: Jesus Christ is the light of the world.

All: The light no darkness can quench.

Play quiet music, from a worship, or classical, tape (e.g. Beethoven's 'Moonlight' Sonata).

Give thanks (slowly, with plenty of pauses) for such matters as:

- *God's love for and welcome of us (Romans 15.7), the name by which we are known;*

- *that we are known and called by name in Christ (Ephesians 1.4);*

- *the new name that is ours in Christ (Revelation 2.17);*

- *that as believers we have taken on the name/character of Christ (Isaiah 62.4);*

- *thank God for each other and for his love for us personally.*

You might wish to ask different people to read out each of the above verses. If so, ask them before, not during, the meeting so that people's listening is not disrupted.

Putting it into practice

Ask everyone to pay attention to their own sense of identity, and to the search for identity that they observe in the lives of people around them, as well as those portrayed through the media, magazines and any other means they come across in the week. Ask them to come ready to begin next week with their observations and illustrations. Become a 'neighbourhood watch' (!), observing the way people seek and express their identity. They will find it helpful to write observations down as soon as they can, and tear out magazine/paper cuttings to bring with them, rather than hope they remember. Ask people to bring a cutting, a story, a testimony, and so on.

Summary and example timings

	mins
Welcome and opening prayer	5
Group exercise: Significant things	10
Input and discussion: The search for identity	15
Bible study and discussion: What's in a name?	15
Bible study and discussion: A new name	10
Group exercise: How do you see yourself?	20
Prayer together	10
Putting it into practice	5

The search for identity

Input and discussion: The search for identity

Identity is knowing who I am. Many people today are uncertain who they are and are not at peace with themselves.

Values and ideals that used to give people identity in our society are changing all the time. Where should we look to find out who we are?

Some influences today (mainly from the East) are saying: 'lose your identity in the greater universe'. Others (from the New Age movement) say: 'look inside yourself more'.

As Christians we believe we find our true identity in who we are in God's sight.

Bible study and discussion: What's in a name?

A lot of identity is stored up in names. Talk together about the following questions:

- *Does anyone have any stories about 'naming'?*

- *Is there a story behind your own name?*

- *Is there a story behind the names you gave to your children?*

Read aloud Genesis 2.19-24.

> So out of the ground the Lord God formed every animal of the field and every bird of the air, and brought them to the man to see what he would call them; and whatever the man called each living creature, that was its name. The man gave names to all cattle, and to the birds of the air, and to every animal of the field; but for the man there was not found a helper as his partner. So the Lord God caused a deep sleep to fall upon the man, and he slept; then he took one of his ribs and closed up its place with flesh. And the rib that the Lord God had taken from the man he made into a woman and brought her to the man. Then the man said, 'This at last is bone of my bones and flesh of my flesh; this one shall be called Woman, for out of man this one was taken.' Therefore a man leaves his father and his mother and clings to his wife, and they become one flesh. And the man and his wife were both naked, and were not ashamed.
>
> Genesis 2.19-24

- *Why didn't God tell Adam the names of the animals? (Would you have chosen a different name for any of them?)*

- *Why is naming things important?*

- *Does anyone have a story about when a doctor named their condition; or a story of the problems of not knowing the names of things or people?*

- *What happens when we get names wrong? Does anyone have a story of a wrong diagnosis by a doctor or car mechanic, etc.?*

- *What happens when names are used destructively? Can you think of examples?*

Bible study and discussion: A new name

As a whole group read aloud Matthew 16.13-20. Explore the impact of Peter's new name.

> Now when Jesus came into the district of Caesarea Philippi, he asked his disciples, 'Who do people say that the Son of Man is?' And they said, 'Some say John the Baptist, but others Elijah, and still others Jeremiah or one of the prophets.' He said to them, 'But who do you say that I am?' Simon Peter answered, 'You are the Messiah, the Son of the living God.' And Jesus answered him, 'Blessed are you, Simon son of Jonah! For flesh and blood has not revealed this to you, but my Father in heaven. And I tell you, you are Peter, and on this rock I will build my church, and the gates of Hades will not prevail against it. I will give you the keys of the kingdom of heaven, and whatever you bind on earth will be bound in heaven, and whatever you loose on earth will be loosed in heaven.' Then he sternly ordered the disciples not to tell anyone that he was the Messiah.
>
> Matthew 16.13-20

- *Make a list together of other people you can think of in Scripture who received a new name.*

- *Explore how Peter 'became' or 'grew into' his new name – through denial, restoration and Pentecost.*

- *Think through the way Peter's identity is continually developing through the Gospels and Acts.*

- *Do you have experience of growing into a new identity in your own Christian life?*

Group exercise: How do you see yourself?

Fold another piece of paper into four. Put the letter 'F' (for female) in the top left-hand corner of the top square and the letter 'M' (for male) in the top right-hand corner.

Write the names of the people who had the most significant influences on you in your growing years (birth to 16). This will not always be your parents. Write the men on one part of the paper and the women on the other.

In the top two squares – under the names – list ways in which you see yourself as being like those you have identified. In the bottom two squares note the ways in which you see yourself as different from them.

In groups of two or three share what this tells you about how you see yourself.

Prayer together

Leader: Jesus Christ is the light of the world;

All: The light that no darkness can quench.

Putting it into practice

Pay attention this week:

- *to your own sense of identity;*

- *to the search of those around you for identity and meaning;*

- *to those portrayed in the media.*

Come next week with observations and illustrations. You may find it helpful to write things down or tear out magazine or paper cuttings.

The search for identity

Introduction

The purpose of the five sessions of this course is to explore what the Bible says about the believer being a new creation in Christ. We will look at the modern search for personal identity (seeking answers to the question 'who am I?'). The aim is to deepen our inner sense of security and well-being so that we can more readily fulfil our calling to love God and others as we love ourselves. Foundational to the whole process is the fact that:

> There can be no love of others, much less love of God, without a self to do the loving.
>
> Roberta Bondi, *To Pray and to Love*

The first session is designed to give some understanding as to why there is a deep search for identity and meaning today, to alert us to some of the dangers in that search and in some of the answers being offered, and to get in touch with our own sense of personal identity.

What is identity?

Identity is my awareness of who I am, my ability to complete the sentence 'I am . . . ', and to be able to be at peace and accept that self that I am aware of. In two ways the modern search for identity tends to be looking in the wrong direction.

We are often looking for something fixed or certain. In a rapidly changing world that is hardly surprising. However, we are alive, growing and changing. Our identity is not fixed, we are becoming people. So our identity is a journey we are on, not a destination we have reached.

Modern culture tends to look for identity as an isolated self-contained entity. Psychology, experience and Scripture all combine to show that identity is found only in relationship to life, other people, the world around us and, as Christians testify, God. It is about a sense of belonging. Identity is less like a house (a fixed, static, measurable building) than it is like a home (the unfolding story of the community that a family is becoming).

Why the modern search?

John Powell's book, *Why Am I Afraid to Tell You Who I Am?* has sold over three million copies. Scott Peck's book, *The Road Less Travelled* was in the top ten bestsellers in America every week for eleven years! Why? Two major causes can be suggested. Partly, it is the result of an affluent society that is no longer exhaustively involved in the search for food and shelter. There is leisure time to consider 'higher' or 'deeper' needs and drives. Partly, it is the result of the collapse of the framework within which identity was virtually taken for granted. God, religion ('thou shalt not . . . '), a clear moral framework ('good girls don't . . . '), and the networks of extended family and local community, gave a sense of stability to life, and a place to belong. Both are major factors in the creation of a sense of identity.

Undermining identity

Two characteristics of modern society have contributed to the loss of a secure personal identity.

One is the *exaltation of doubt* in our scientific culture. Science proceeds by asking 'Why?' and 'How?' and saying things like 'Prove it!', 'How do you know?', 'What is the evidence?' They are valid questions. Without them penicillin would not have been discovered or the microchip invented. However, this 'culture of suspicion', as it has been called, creates havoc when applied to personal relationships. You cannot 'prove' that anyone loves you. You cannot even prove you exist!

The other is the way our culture *enshrines rebellion*. Heresy is literally 'standing against' the community and its norms. Historically all cultures have had such norms and values, which are the glue that holds a community together, gives it its identity, and so feeds the identity of the individuals in it. Such values are often enshrined in heroes (people we can 'identify with'). However, our culture has turned that pattern upside down. Today, identity is found by standing out from the crowd and by rejecting anything that might pass for a norm or pattern. This can be seen in the rejection of 'heroes'. They function as symbols of the values of society. Today's heroes are anti-heroes; whose identity is expressed by being 'against' and 'apart' from everyone else. It is a hard act to perform, and a harder act to follow.

False trails

Two approaches to finding identity are frequently advocated today.

The first is to *lose your identity*. This is the path of Eastern mysticism, which sees the individual as a drop in the ocean whose goal is to become one with the ocean, losing all sense of self.

The second is to *look within*. This is evident in New Age teaching about 'I am my own divinity', using texts such as 'The Father and I are one' to mean 'I am my own spiritual source'.

This course explores the alternative, Christian, route to personal identity, namely that *looking outwards* to love God and others is how we best find ourselves.

The gift of identity

There are a number of verses from Scripture referred to in the members' handout. Come with a Bible to read them or, better still, invite others to share in this work.

You will also need enough A4 sheets of paper for each person present.

Welcome and opening prayer

The person who welcomes the group and begins the meeting with prayer should read the following sentence in a moment of quiet:

> To be a Christian is to believe that it is the Father who defines our identity and is to be believed against all the inner and outer accusations to the contrary when he says to us 'This child of mine'.
>
> Tom Smail, *The Forgotten Father*

Reporting back

Discuss together the work you agreed to do on last session's 'Putting it into practice'.

Input and discussion: Finding my identity in Christ

Spend a little time reminding people of the modern problem of the search for identity (see last session's supplementary handout (pp. 76–7). Then introduce the four cornerstones of Christian identity. An outline is on the members' handout with further background in the supplementary handout for this session (pp. 73–7).

The Bible gives us a firm place on which to establish who we are. There are four cornerstones making up the Christian personal identity. These cornerstones are God's gift – open to all humanity.

We are made in the image of God

We can easily feel very insignificant in the face of the vastness of the universe. God created the heavens and the earth and he gave us a key place in the creation: we are dearly loved by him (Psalm 8.3-4). According to Psalm 139 God made us as unique individuals.

We are adopted as children of God

The gospel is about restoring the image of God that has been broken and spoiled by our going it alone. Now, in Christ, God has become our Father, giving us his identity and calling us his children (Romans 8.15-16).

We are called by name

God gives each of his people a new name – individual to us. He has a personal call on our life. He made us different from everyone else and gives us different gifts and ministries (Revelation 2.17).

We are indwelt by Christ

God lives in us. We find our true identity when Christ is enthroned at the centre of our life (Colossians 1.27; Galatians 2.20).

After the input, invite the group to share:

■   *what rings true to their experience (encouraging them to tell their relevant stories);*

■   *what has spoken to them (as something that helps them understand their experience);*

■   *what they are not clear or remain puzzled about. (Do not let this dominate.)*

Bible study and discussion: The new self

Read Ephesians 4.17-32. (Text is on members' handouts)

As for the children of Israel, there is an exodus taking place here, a journey, out of a diseased way of seeing ourselves and living life, into the promised land of life lived in the strength, presence, and dynamic of Christ.

Ask the group to look at the passage in (twos or threes) and work out what it is saying about the old way of life and the new. See suggested questions on the handout on p. 74. After everyone has had some time to work on the passage, together reflect on and share your thoughts about the marks of the two ways of life.

Encourage people to explore together where they see themselves on this exodus – and in what ways they have taken steps forward during the *Emmaus* course.

Group exercise: Becoming a new person

See the members' handout for the details of this exercise.

Meditation

Pray together following the pattern you have established as a group.

Putting it into practice

Ask the group to take time in silence to consider, and note accordingly, any obstacles to your receiving the gift of a new identity in Christ, and steps you can take to receive such a gift. What practical steps can we take to live in the truth of how God sees us?

If time allows, you may want to work together in twos or threes to help each other identify the obstacles, and plan the steps.

Summary and example timings

	mins
Welcome and opening prayer	5
Reporting back	10
Input and discussion: Finding my identity in Christ	20
Bible study and discussion: The new self	20
Group exercise: Becoming a new person	20
Meditation	10
Putting it into practice	5

The gift of identity

Reporting back

In threes share how your action plan worked out this week – successes and failures. Especially report:

- *any changes in your own self-understanding and acceptance;*

- *any observations of those around you or in the media.*

Input and discussion: Finding my identity in Christ

The Bible gives us a firm place on which to establish who we are. There are four cornerstones to the Christian personal identity it provides. These cornerstones are God's gift – open to all humanity.

We are made in the image of God

We often feel very insignificant in the face of the vastness of the universe. God created the heavens and the earth and he gave us a key place in the creation: we are dearly loved by him (Psalm 8.3-4). According to Psalm 139 God made us as unique individuals.

We are adopted as God's children

The gospel is about restoring the image of God that has been broken and spoiled by our going it alone. Now, in Christ, God has become our Father, giving us his identity and calling us his children (Romans 8.15-16).

We are called by name

God gives each of his people a new name – individual to us. He has a personal call on our life. He made us different from everyone else and gives us different gifts and ministries (Revelation 2.17).

We are indwelt by Christ

God lives in us. We find our true identity when Christ is enthroned at the centre of our life (Colossians 1.27; Galatians 2.20).

- *What rings true to your experience?*

- *What speaks to you?*

- *What are you still puzzled about?*

Bible study and discussion: The new self

> Now this I affirm and insist on in the Lord: you must no longer live as the Gentiles live, in the futility of their minds. They are darkened in their understanding, alienated from the life of God because of their ignorance and hardness of heart. They have lost all sensitivity and have abandoned themselves to licentiousness, greedy to practise every kind of impurity. That is not the way you learned Christ! For surely you have heard about him and were taught in him, as truth is in Jesus. You were taught to put away your former way of life, your old self, corrupt and deluded by its lusts, and to be renewed in the spirit of your minds, and to clothe yourselves with the new self, created according to the likeness of God in true righteousness and holiness.
>
> So then, putting away falsehood, let all of us speak the truth to our neighbours, for we are members of one another. Be angry but do not sin; do not let the sun go down on your anger, and do not make room for the devil. Thieves must give up stealing; rather let them labour and work honestly with their own hands, so as to have something to share with the needy. Let no evil talk come out of your mouths, but only what is useful for building up, as there is need, so that your words may give grace to those who hear. And do not grieve the Holy Spirit of God, with which you were marked with a seal for the day of redemption. Put away from you all bitterness and wrath and anger and wrangling and slander, together with all malice, and be kind to one another, tenderhearted, forgiving one another, as God in Christ has forgiven you.
>
> Ephesians 4.17-32

Paul is describing a change in who we are in Christ – a journey from the old to the new.

The Ephesians were taught:

- *to put off the old self;*
- *to be made new in their attitudes;*
- *to put on the new self.*

Can you identify from the passage and your own observations on life the characteristics of the old self and the new?

Share together what you think Paul means by any of these three things. Make your examples practical and real.

Group exercise: Becoming a new person

Take a piece of paper (A4, 'portrait') and draw a cup-sized circle in the middle. Fold the paper (across, not down, the page) and in the top half of the circle write your name.

Draw bubbles coming out of the centre circle and put a characteristic of yourself in each bubble. In this way we can begin to define the shape of the person we see God bringing into being in us, and calling out of us. We may only see the seedlings now, but ask God to give us a vision of the person we are becoming. Share this in pairs and threes.

Now, in quiet prayer, ask God for the gift of a new name for the person you are becoming:

■   *it may be an actual name, which defines a character;*

■   *or a phrase ('loved by God', 'strong in Christ', 'precious in his sight');*

■   *or a character from history or from literature ('Valiant for truth', or 'Columba');*

■   *or simply a character description ('faithful', 'bold', 'generous').*

Write down this name, word or phrase in the lower half of the circle.

Share these insights with each other; help each other where the picture is not yet clear. Assist and suggest, do not impose or press.

Putting it into practice

Consider, and note accordingly, any obstacles to your receiving the gift of a new identity in Christ, and steps you can take to receive such a gift. What practical steps can we take to live in the truth of how God sees us?

The gift of identity

Introduction

Modern humanity is all at sea about its identity. What is more, our own culture has thrown away the charts of its Christian heritage by which to find our way home. We are doubly adrift.

Staying with the watery picture, the Psalmist gives his testimony to God's grace in these words:

> I waited patiently for the Lord;
> he inclined to me and heard my cry.
> He drew me up from the desolate pit.
> out of the miry bog,
> and set my feet upon a rock,
> making my steps secure.
> He put a new song in my mouth,
> a song of praise to our God.
> Many will see and fear,
> and put their trust in the Lord.
>
> Psalm 40.1-3

Scripture gives us the firm place on which to establish our identity and the home of self-understanding and self-acceptance, in which we can find a secure place to live. There are four cornerstones to this Christian personal identity. They are God's gift open to all humanity.

Made in the image of God

One of the downsides of modern scientific discoveries, and perhaps particularly the discoveries about the vastness of space, is just how small and insignificant we human beings are. The Psalmist (Psalm 8.3-4) felt like that, even before modern discoveries, no doubt simply as a result of looking at the star-covered canopy of space on a cloudless (and street-lightless!) night:

> When I look at your heavens, the work of your fingers,
> the moon and the stars that you have established;
> what are human beings that you are mindful of them,
> mortals that you care for them?
>
> Psalm 8.3-4

The answer the Psalmist gives is not how insignificant we are, but how loved we are. That love is founded on the uniqueness of our human existence and nature. We are made in the image of God. There are many aspects of that image to which we can point. Our ability to think and reason, and express thoughts in language. Our ability to make moral choices, to give love. Our ability to be creative, to be original. Yet undergirding all these is simply the fact that we are made as persons after the order of a personal God. In fact the word 'person' was first used by theologians trying to describe the nature of God at the time of the writing of the creeds of the Church. Only later did psychologists pick up the word to describe human nature.

Everyone, even the most depraved, reflects something of God's nature.

Adopted as God's children

The gospel is about restoring the image of God that has been broken and marred by our going it alone. Now, in Christ, God has become our Father – giving us his identity – and calling us his children. 'Not as orphans are we left in sorrow now', as the hymn puts it. As Paul says:

> You have received a spirit of adoption. When we cry, 'Abba! Father!' it is
> that very Spirit bearing witness with our spirit that we are children of God.
>
> Romans 8.15-16

Called by name

Wonderful though it is to be a creature before the Creator, made in his image and adopted as his children, there is yet more that gives and enriches our identity. There is a personal call on our lives. Names are so important, as the new names like Abraham for Abram, Peter for Simon and Paul for Saul, testify.

There are various names by which God calls us. 'Beloved' is a special one. It is from the image of marriage (see Psalm 40, Song of Songs, Ephesians 5.32 and Revelation 19.7). It is a truth to drink in, and to take delight in, that this is how God sees us. He has also given us the name 'Christ' (this was why the term 'Christian' stuck), seeing us 'in Christ' as he sees Jesus. He also addresses us with a new name that expresses the identity that results from being found in him (Revelation 2.17).

Indwelt by Christ

The deepest inner truth about believers is that God lives in them. Some Orthodox icons portray the saints with their heart opened and Christ enthroned within. Modern humanity's search for identity puts the self in the place of Christ. This indwelling is the work of the Holy Spirit, both through creation when God breathed into us the breath of life, and at Pentecost when the Spirit came to dwell within believers. There is a progression in God's self-disclosure at this point. The Exodus expressed God-for-us, the incarnation God-with-us, and Pentecost God-in-us. Paul expresses this indwelling of Christ in defining his gospel as 'Christ in you, the hope of glory' (Colossians 1.27), and by testifying to his own experience as 'Christ lives in me' (Galatians 2.20).

Practising Christ's presence

As Christians we are called to walk by faith, not by sight – or by feelings. This means affirming the truth of God's word about us and exalting that above 'how I feel today'. This means that we need to draw strength from this four-fold foundation – daily. Doing so is what is meant by practising the Presence of Christ. It is really a 'renewal of consciousness'. We need to thank God for the truth about ourselves as made in his image, adopted as his child, called 'Beloved', and indwelt by Christ. Each of us is to do this personally. In fellowship together, we can share how we do this, hear how others practise such a daily renewal of consciousness and work together to live out of this secure sense of being and well-being.

The model of identity

Welcome and opening prayer

As in previous weeks, invite another member of the group to prepare and lead this part of the meeting, perhaps sharing something of what they have received through the course so far.

Reporting back

Report on the results of 'Putting into practice' the plans from last week about receiving the gift of a new identity in Christ and overcoming obstacles to receive his gifts. Share successes in order to encourage each other. Also share failures, both so that we can work on the problems together, and so that others can be encouraged by the fact that we don't have to succeed all the time!

Input and discussion: Looking at Jesus

Again, give an introduction to this session's theme, based around the following points (which are reproduced on the members' handout for the session). Use the supplementary handout either to go into the topic in more depth with the whole group or for your own background reading (see pp. 83–4).

Where can we look for our model and picture of what it means to be human?

Jesus is the one whole human being who has ever lived. He is the living image of his Father. He offers that gift to us.

Jesus finds his identity in knowing who he is – the Son of God, loved by his Father.

At his baptism he does not receive a task to do, so much as an affirmation of who he is:

> You are my Son, the Beloved; with you I am well pleased.
>
> Luke 3.22

Identity for us is not the result of a search within but the fruit of knowing we are loved.

The first task of Jesus' life is to be someone, not to do something.

Identity for us comes by receiving 'who we are' as a gift. It is not something we achieve by doing or by achieving.

Because he was secure in his being, Jesus was free for astonishing doing. He gave the ultimate gift of himself in death.

As we become secure in our identity we are able to live and give effectively.

Invite group members to comment on:

- *what rings true to their experience (encouraging them to tell their relevant stories);*

- *what has spoken to them (as something that helps them understand their experience);*

- *what they are not clear or remain puzzled about. (Do not let this dominate.)*

Bible study and discussion: Jesus, you and me

Read Luke 2.46-52 with Luke 3.21-22.

Have a few minutes for silent reflection before inviting people to share reflections about:

- *evidences of Jesus' good self-image;*

- *clues as to where he got that from.*

Do not discuss, other than to ask for clarification; simply get people to put thoughts 'on the table'.

Then, in the light of both passages and comments 'tabled', invite responses as to:

- *what this has to say to us;*

- *in what ways this links up with our own personal experience/observation of life.*

Group exercise: Describing ourselves

This exercise works best with groups of four, but it can be done with threes (and fives) too.

Ask someone to start by telling a story about something they did/tackled recently, which they enjoyed doing or had a sense of achievement in doing.

Explain to others in the group that their task is to listen so that at the end of the story they can say what characteristics and what skills they see the person expressing or exercising in that event.

Repeat this for each person in turn.

In pairs (or in the group of four or the whole group) ask people to share what they have learned about themselves.

Meditation

Repeat and develop the pattern of the first session.

It will probably be important to pick up on the themes of the Bible study and the exercise in the prayer time for this session.

Give some time, space and encouragement to people to offer to God their own picture of themselves – and to receive from him afresh that new identity in God.

Some form of prayer that enables the group to take off the old self and put on the new may be helpful.

Putting it into practice

First, in your prayer life, develop a short, set form of prayer that writes the truth about us, as God sees us, into your innermost thinking. Two possible forms of this 'liturgy of the heart' are:

> The God of the universe celebrates my existence.

or

> In Christ I am chosen and loved for eternity.

It may well be best for each of us to develop our own particular way of receiving the truth of God about the 'new self, created according to the likeness of God in true righteousness and holiness' (Ephesians 4.24). Be open to that, while still using one of the above until you have developed your own.

Second, in your personal relationships, look for opportunities to affirm the people with whom you live and work and play. It is good to affirm actions – what people do – but better still to affirm (which means 'to make strong') who people are. Come next week ready to share your joys and struggles in the practice of affirmation.

Summary and example timings

	mins
Welcome and opening prayer	5
Reporting back	10
Input and discussion: Looking at Jesus	20
Bible study and discussion: Jesus, you and me	20
Group exercise: Describing ourselves	20
Meditation	10
Putting it into practice	5

The model of identity

Reporting back

Share the results of putting into practice the plans from last week about receiving the gift of a new identity in Christ, and overcoming obstacles to receive his gifts.

Share successes in order to encourage each other.

Also share failures, both so that we can work on the problems together, and so that others can be encouraged by the fact that we don't have to succeed all the time!

Input and discussion: Looking at Jesus

Where can we look for our model and picture of what it means to be human?

Jesus is the one whole human being who has ever lived. He is the living image of his Father. He offers that gift to us.

Jesus finds his identity in knowing who he is – the Son of God, loved by his Father.

At his baptism, he does not receive a task to do but an affirmation of who he is:

> You are my Son, the Beloved; with you I am well pleased.
>
> Luke 3.22

Identity for us is not the result of a search within but the fruit of knowing we are loved.

The first task of Jesus' life is to be someone, not to do something.

Identity for us comes by receiving 'who we are' as a gift. It is not something we achieve by doing or by achieving.

Because he was secure in his being, Jesus was free for astonishing doing. He gave the ultimate gift of himself in death.

As we become secure in our identity we are able to live and give effectively.

Bible study and discussion: Jesus, you and me

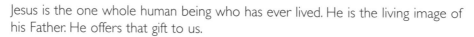

> After three days they found him in the temple, sitting among the teachers, listening to them and asking them questions. And all who heard him were amazed at his understanding and his answers. When his parents saw him they were astonished; and his mother said to him, 'Child, why have you treated us like this? Look, your father and I have been searching for you in great anxiety.' He said to them, 'Why were you searching for me? Did you not know that I must be in my Father's house?' But they did not understand what he said to them. Then he went down with them and came to Nazareth, and was obedient to them. His mother treasured all these things in her heart.
>
> And Jesus increased in wisdom and in years, and in divine and human favour.
>
> Luke 2.46-52

> Now when all the people were baptized, and when Jesus also had been baptized and was praying, the heaven was opened, and the Holy Spirit descended upon him in bodily form like a dove. And a voice came from heaven, 'You are my Son, the Beloved; with you I am well pleased.'
>
> Luke 3.21-22

Share your reflections about:

■ *evidences of Jesus' good self-image;*

■ *clues as to where he got that from.*

When you have listened to everyone's contribution, think together about:

■ *What does this have to say to us?*

■ *In what ways does this link up with our own personal experience/observation of life?*

Group exercise: Describing ourselves

Each of us in turn (though anyone does, of course, have the right not to take part) is asked to tell a story about something we have recently done/achieved/tackled, which we enjoyed doing or had a sense of achievement in doing, or felt good about doing.

While we are telling our story, the other members of the group will be watching out for any characteristics that they saw us expressing in that story and any skills they saw us exercising in that event.

When we have finished our story the group will then tell us what they saw.

We then repeat this exercise for each person of the group in turn.

We can then share what we have learned about through this exercise.

Meditation

Spend some time in quiet prayer together, either in pairs or as a whole group.

Putting it into practice

Practise praying about your identity in Christ. Write a prayer or find a Scripture that you can use. And practise affirming other people around you; about who they are and what their gifts are.

The model of identity

Introduction

Before going on to consider further, in the next two sessions, how we are to live in the truth of the identity that is ours as creatures and children of the living God, we pause in this middle session to consider Jesus. He is the one whole human being who has ever lived. In his life we see true, healthy, God-given identity being lived out. He was the living image of his Father. The good news is that he has opened up that gift to us.

In this session we explore how Jesus lived out the truths we considered last session, that human beings are made in God's image, adopted into his family, and called by name.

Called by name – at his baptism

The baptism of Jesus was a remarkable event. It represented his commissioning or ordination. As such we might expect the sermon (the 'word' that comes from the Father) to be about the job in hand. In part, the hidden part, it is; for the 'word' that comes from heaven is a combination of two Old Testament scriptures. One points to his being 'great David's greater Son', with great kingly authority (Psalm 2.7), and the other to his calling to follow the path of the suffering servant, as outlined in Isaiah's 'servant songs' (Isaiah 42.1). But those truths are hidden below the surface. What lies so clearly above the surface is the affirmation of who he is – in the Father's love.

> You are my Son, the Beloved; with you I am well pleased.
>
> Luke 3.22

Jesus begins, continues and ends his life and ministry from the security of knowing he is loved by God. As God calls him the Beloved, he sees and speaks of God as Abba, Father. So too, for us, identity is the result not of a search within, but rather the fruit of knowing we are loved.

Living by grace – throughout his life

Wonderful though such an affirmation is, it seems a little strange in the context of commission for service, which is what Jesus' baptism was. Or, it seems strange until we realize that the first task of Jesus' life was to be someone, rather than do something. Not that you can isolate 'being' and 'doing' into separate compartments. One is expressed in the other.

However, what we see in Jesus is that the doing arises out of who he was. Who he was arose not out of his looking within, or out of his trying to find or create his own identity, but out of his being given identity by God. He is sustained through life by intimacy with, and confidence (faith) in, the Father who loved him.

The modern search for identity usually goes the wrong way round at this point. It is something I achieve, or find; rather than something I receive because I have been found. Moreover, we so easily try to find our identity (being) through our doing. That doing takes many forms. Trying to achieve something great, making money or a reputation for ourselves, or making ourselves attractive – sexually, socially or by always pleasing people and by only doing and saying 'nice' things. But every attempt to achieve identity fails. It comes by receiving it as a gift – and then going out to live in the generosity of that gift.

Giving as good as he got – even in death

Because he was secure in his being, Jesus was free for astonishing doing. He was able to give or withhold, enjoy or abstain, be still or be energetic as the moment required – or rather, as he heard from God in each moment. So, although he comes to the well where the Samaritan woman is, tired and thirsty (John 4.6-7), he listens to the Father, speaks a word that is life-giving to the woman, and then finds, when the disciples return with food, that he is already refreshed:

> My food is to do the will of him who sent me and to complete his work.
>
> John 4.34

Because of this security in his identity as the Beloved Son, Jesus could live as a creature before the Creator, without becoming focused on created things or making idols of them.

> To depend on God is to be free of men, things and self. It is to be able to take pleasure in all his gifts without being the slave of any. It is to be able, as occasion demands, to spend and save, to speak and to forbear, to act and to rest, to be grave and gay, to defend oneself and to surrender.
>
> Paul Tournier, *The Meaning of Persons*

The ultimate gift is himself, in death. This is not something forced out of him but a freely given gift: 'No one takes it from me, but I lay it down of my own accord' (John 10.18).

Living images of the Father

This is the life we are called to through our baptism into Christ. We have received a new identity, that of being adopted as God's children. It is this security that sustains us through all the ups and downs in life. It is this identity that enables us, as it did Jesus, both to take proper authority to control and shape life (and say 'no' to others), and yet also to respond in waiting, in giving way, in giving ourselves; as we discern God's call in each situation.

The battle for identity

You will need enough A4 sheets of paper for each person present.

Welcome and opening prayer

As in previous sessions, invite another member of the group to prepare and lead this part of the meeting, perhaps sharing something of what they have received through the course so far.

Reporting back

In pairs or threes share the successes and struggles you have experienced in praying prayers of affirmation and in affirming others. Work out together how to take this practice forward, correcting mistakes, overcoming obstacles and building on successes. Encourage the group to keep going with this. Building up good habits can take as long as giving up bad ones.

Input and discussion: Understanding the battle

Give an introduction to this session's theme, based around the following points (which are reproduced on the members' handout for the session). Use the supplementary handout either to go into the topic in more depth with the whole group or for your own background reading (see pp. 92–3).

How is our identity formed?

Our identity is made up of and formed by a number of different elements:

■ *the rich mosaic of life: where we are born, who our parents are, what is 'given' to us;*

■ *the choices we make along the way;*

■ *a focusing instinct: the hunger for a focus of interest that will give meaning to life. Worship of God rightly expresses this. Without God, anything else becomes an idol.*

Conversion

Conversion is the movement and moment through which God becomes the focus and centre and organizing principle of life.

To be a disciple is to be one who daily says: 'I turn to Christ; I repent of my sins; I renounce evil.' Here lies the battle.

A new creation

The Bible speaks of a battle within us between our old nature (on the one side) and the Spirit of God establishing our new nature (on the other).

Christians have often emphasized the battle against the old nature and the need to put to death our old selves. But we sometimes lose sight of what the new nature is meant to be.

Living in the new creation

For all Christians this is a continual process:

■   *putting to death the old nature;*

■   *affirming the new nature.*

Invite group members to comment on:

■   *what rings true to their experience (encouraging them to tell their relevant stories);*

■   *what has spoken to them as something that helps them understand their experience;*

■   *what they are not clear or remain puzzled about. (Do not let this dominate.)*

Bible study and discussion: The battle within

Read Romans 8.5-17.

Invite someone to pray a prayer of invitation to the Holy Spirit to come and inspire the listening as he inspired the writing. (Christians believe in this double inspiration of Scripture.)

Take five minutes in silence for everyone to listen to the passage, making a note of any word, phrase, or thought that speaks to you.

Go round the room inviting each person (while giving freedom for anyone to say 'pass') to contribute their insights. Do not discuss or argue, simply ask for clarification or express appreciation for what people have said, and get the group to take the same attitude.

Group exercise: Describing our journey

One way of doing this is to give people a piece of A4 paper and ask them to:

■   *hold it in front of them in landscape rather than portrait form (long side as base of paper);*

■   *draw a path wending its way from the bottom left-hand corner to the top right-hand corner of the paper;*

■   *in the top left-hand corner of the paper write 'joys', and in the bottom right-hand corner write 'struggles'.*

The task is to plot on this path ways in which you have been aware of growing as a person in recent months (or years). The idea is to plot milestones, turning points, vital moments, or simply phases or stages of that journey, e.g. starting a new job or relationship, divorce, difficult decision, new task taken on, etc. Note down the event on the path you have drawn, with the first event near the bottom left-hand corner, and the most recent near the top right-hand corner.

Above the path (in the 'joys' part) make a note of:

■   *any way you feel you have grown through this experience (with words like 'confidence', 'courage', etc.).*

Below the path (in the 'struggle' part) make a note of:

■   *any way in which you feel you have struggled, and if you can, identify the thing that you are struggling with (using words like 'fear', 'lack of self-confidence', etc.).*

Allow about ten minutes for people to draw this, and then to explain their journey to each other in groups of two or three.

Remember that points of struggle (the Cross) are very often the way through (to new life); so, in the context of this session, it is good to talk about the battle for a wholesome identity that we have experienced through the events we have been through recently.

Meditation

Follow the instruction and pattern of the previous occasions, but this time invite prayer contributions from all – but in the form of:

Thanksgivings

- *for our being made, and remade, in God's image;*

- *for our being accepted in Christ;*

- *for the grace to know and choose God's will.*

Affirmations

- *of God's presence with us;*

- *of his image in us;*

- *of his goodness to us.*

Conclude with the prayer:

Almighty God,
who wonderfully created us in your own image
and yet more wonderfully restored us
through your Son Jesus Christ:
grant that, as he came to share in our humanity,
so we may share the life of his divinity;
who is alive and reigns with you,
in the unity of the Holy Spirit,
one God, now and for ever. Amen.

Common Worship: Collect for the First Sunday of Christmas

Putting it into practice

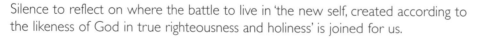

Lead straight from the previous section into:

Silence to reflect on where the battle to live in 'the new self, created according to the likeness of God in true righteousness and holiness' is joined for us.

Note a personal issue that needs working on.

Identify one or two actions to take in the coming week, in the light of the above.

In threes, share what has emerged (including one's action plan), and encourage one another in choosing God's way in life, avoiding being experts and giving advice. Give acceptance and support. Pray for each other, giving God's blessing to one another (Numbers 6.24-26), which is itself a means of affirming others and strengthening their self-acceptance.

Also encourage people to give affirmation to others, and give away to Christians and non-Christians alike the good things that you have grasped so far. The best way to get hold of the truth is to give it away to others.

Summary and example timings

	mins
Welcome and opening prayer	5
Reporting back	10
Input and discussion: Understanding the battle	20
Bible study and discussion: The battle within	15
Group exercise: Describing our journey	20
Meditation	10
Putting it into practice	10

The battle for identity

Reporting back

Share the successes and struggles you have experienced in praying prayers of affirmation, and in affirming others. Work out together how to take this practice forward, correcting mistakes, overcoming obstacles and building on your own and others' successes.

Input and discussion: Understanding the battle

Our identity is made up and formed by a number of different elements:

■ *the rich mosaic of life: where we are born, who our parents are, what is 'given' to us;*

■ *the choices we make along the way;*

■ *a focusing instinct: the hunger for a focus of interest that will give meaning to life. Worship of God rightly expresses this. Without God, anything else becomes an idol.*

Conversion

Conversion is the movement and moment through which God becomes the focus and centre and organizing principle of life.

To be a disciple is to be one who daily says: 'I turn to Christ; I repent of my sins; I renounce evil'. Here lies the battle.

A new creation

The Bible speaks of a battle within us between our old nature (on the one side) and the Spirit of God establishing our new nature (on the other).

Christians have often emphasized the battle against the old nature and the need to put to death our old selves. But we sometimes lose sight of what the new nature is meant to be.

Living in the new creation

For all Christians this is a continual process:

■ *putting to death the old nature;*

■ *affirming the new nature.*

Bible study and discussion: The battle within

For those who live according to the flesh set their minds on the things of the flesh, but those who live according to the Spirit set their minds on the things of the Spirit. To set the mind on the flesh is death, but to set the mind on the Spirit is life and peace. For this reason the mind that is set on the flesh is hostile to God; it does not submit to God's law – indeed it cannot, and those who are in the flesh cannot please God.

But you are not in the flesh; you are in the Spirit, since the Spirit of God dwells in you. Anyone who does not have the Spirit of Christ does not belong to him. But if Christ is in you, though the body is dead because of sin, the Spirit is life because of righteousness. If the Spirit of him who raised Jesus from the dead dwells in you, he who raised Christ from the dead will give life to your mortal bodies also through his Spirit that dwells in you.

So then, brothers and sisters, we are debtors, not to the flesh, to live according to the flesh – for if you live according to the flesh, you will die; but if by the Spirit you put to death the deeds of the body, you will live. For all who are led by the Spirit of God are children of God. For you did not receive a spirit of slavery to fall back into fear; but you have received a spirit of adoption. When we cry, 'Abba! Father!' it is that very Spirit bearing witness with our spirit that we are children of God, and if children, then heirs with Christ – if, in fact, we suffer with him so that we may also be glorified with him.

Romans 8.5-17

After listening to the passage being read, take time, in silence, to note any word, phrase or thought that comes to you. There will be a chance to share these with the group.

Group exercise: Describing our journey

The task is to plot on this path ways in which we have been aware of growing as a person in recent months (or years). The idea is to plot milestones, turning points, vital moments, or simply phases or stages of that journey – e.g. starting a new job or relationship, divorce, difficult decision, new task taken on, etc.

Can you identify any way you feel you have grown through this experience (such as gaining confidence, courage, etc.).

Can you identify any way in which you feel you have struggled, and, if you can, identify the thing that you were struggling with (such as through fear, lack of self-confidence, etc.).

Meditation

Share prayers together especially on the themes of:

Thanksgivings

■ *for our being made, and remade, in God's image;*

■ *for our being accepted in Christ;*

■ *for the grace to know and choose God's will.*

Affirmations

■ *of God's presence with us;*

■ *his image in us;*

■ *his goodness to us.*

> Almighty God,
> who wonderfully created us in your own image
> and yet more wonderfully restored us
> through your Son Jesus Christ:
> grant that, as he came to share in our humanity,
> so we may share the life of his divinity;
> who is alive and reigns with you,
> in the unity of the Holy Spirit
> one God, now and for ever. Amen.
>
> *Common Worship*: Collect for the First Sunday of Christmas

Putting it into practice

In threes, share a plan to put into action what you have learned. Encourage one another in choosing God's way in life. Pray for each other, giving God's blessing to one another.

The battle for identity

Introduction

In the first session we looked at some of the modern distortions in the search for personal identity. But there are deeper distortions that belong to human nature throughout history. The Bible calls the fundamental cause sin: our 'determination to manage by ourselves'. This means that there is a battle in the soul of each person. To understand this more, and to engage with this spiritual battle, we need to know more about how our identity is formed.

Forming identity

The rich mosaic of life is involved in the formation of our identity. From the colour of my hair to the number of siblings I grew up with, from the circumstances of my mother's pregnancy to my playground experiences, and from the quality of relationship with my parents to my reaction to my first fall from a bicycle, all contribute to the shaping of who I am.

Personal choices contribute profoundly to who we are, and how we see ourselves, which is why two people brought up in similar circumstances sometimes become very different people. My identity is not just about what has happened to me, but how I responded to life.

A focusing instinct shapes everyone's identity. We look for patterns and for an integrating centre to life. We need a focus to make sense of life, giving it meaning and purpose. Worship is the true expression of this instinct. Its distortion is the root of all addictions; whether to substances (alcohol and drugs, etc.), processes (work, shopping, etc.) or relationships (the need to achieve and the need to be liked are both manifestations of 'relationship addictions'). The Bible defines such distorted focusing of life as idolatry.

> My god is that which
> rivets my attention
> centres my activities,
> preoccupies my mind
> and motivates my action.
>
> Luke T. Johnson, *Sharing Possessions*

Conversion

Conversion is the movement and moment through which God becomes the focus, centre, and organizing principle of life. He, and our relationship with him, becomes that which gives meaning, significance and order to life. Moreover, this is not just a step of conversion at the beginning of the life of discipleship, this is discipleship. To be a disciple is to be one who daily says 'I turn to Christ', 'I repent of my sins' and 'I renounce evil'. Herein lies the battle.

A new creation

Scripture, and especially the apostle Paul, speaks of the battle within as a battle between two ages, this age (the world organized without reference to God) and the age to come (the world ordered around the presence, goodness and will of God). It also speaks about the flesh, the old nature and the first Adam on the debit side; and the Spirit (witnessing to our spirit), the new person in Christ and the second (life-giving) Adam.

Sadly the Church has often so emphasized the old nature, and the call to put to death the deeds of the flesh, that the new nature has been lost sight of.

> The soul, with its new centre in Christ, radically changed and redirected, is to be accepted ... This new, real self is largely ignored, feared or even denied ... For the 'walk in the Spirit' the true self is required ... for we become as we remain in Christ, a state of God-consciousness.
>
> Leanne Payne, *The Healing Presence*

Moreover, it has tended to draw the battle lines between 'flesh and spirit' in an unbiblical way: between physical, material things (not least our sexuality) and spiritual things like prayer and worship. The Bible does not support such a false division. Sex can be holy and an expression of the goodness of God. Prayer can be dishonouring to God (remember the Pharisee and the Publican at prayer). The divide is not between material and spiritual, but between me-centred and God-centred living, in the handling of the whole of life.

Living in the new creation

This involves three steps.

First, understanding the source of the battle. Romans, especially chapters 5 to 8, works out the full implications of the battle, as do Ephesians 4, Colossians 3, and 2 Corinthians 5.16-21.

Second, put to death the old nature. We can do this as we identify the diseased attitudes of self-rejection, pride and hostility to others that lurk behind our outward actions. Keeping a journal in which we record these false attitudes (like 'I'm no good', 'I'm stupid') and discovering God's answer to such assaults of the 'accuser of the brethren' (Revelation 12.10) is a vital work.

Third, affirming the new nature. Paul speaks about putting on Christ and the new nature in Colossians 3 and in Ephesians 4. This is the discipline of renewing our minds in God's truth, and in particular the truth about the new identity that is ours in Christ – as defined in Session 2 on the gift of a new identity.

> Be renewed in the spirit of your minds; and ... clothe yourselves with the new self, created according to the likeness of God in true righteousness and holiness.
>
> Ephesians 4.23-24

Living beyond the search for identity

Welcome and opening prayer

As in previous weeks, invite another member of the group to prepare and lead this part of the meeting, perhaps sharing something of what they have received through the course so far.

Reporting back

In threes, share how your 'Putting it into practice' from the end of the last session worked out – successes and failures, any changes in your own self-understanding and acceptance, including any ways in which others may have commented.

Also, share any ways in which you have been able to give what you have received to others and any ways you intend to keep on working at this aspect of identity.

Input and discussion: Freedom from self-concern

Give an introduction to this session's theme, based around the following points (which are reproduced on the members' handout for the session). Use the supplementary handout either to go into the topic in more depth with the whole group or for your own background reading (see pp. 100–101).

Many people are searching for their identity in different ways. Too often the result of that search for identity is becoming obsessed with yourself.

The Bible teaches us that we find our identity when we seek the good of others.

Especially we become free from self-concern and find ourselves in four ways:

Identity in belonging

We find our identity in being part of the body of Christ, the Church – an instrument in an orchestra, not a complete sound in ourselves.

Identity in listening

Our identity takes shape and grows as we listen to God and act in response to his call to us. This is what it means to follow Jesus and be part of the Church, the called people of God.

Identity in living

God has given us 'richly . . . everything for our enjoyment' (1 Timothy 6.17). Jesus came that we might have life in all its fullness (John 10.10). Life involves the enjoyment of creation, social life and the full range of human culture.

Identity in loving

We find our identity when we forget about ourselves and pay attention to God, others and the world.

Check after each point that people understand what you are saying. These are vital truths – but may not be grasped at a first hearing. The more examples you can give, the better.

Then invite group members to comment on:

- *what rings true to their experience (encouraging them to tell their relevant stories);*

- *what has spoken to them (as something that helps them understand their experience);*

- *what they are not clear or remain puzzled about. (Do not let this dominate.)*

Bible study and discussion: From the old to the new

Read Luke 15.11-24 (included in the members' handout).

Here is another 'exodus' (or Emmaus) journey. The journey into the far country is the journey into a false identity.

In the light of the passage and thinking about identity, ask the group to share together their own journey into (or, chasing after) the false self.

In the discussion that follows draw out these points:

Coming to his senses involves the younger son's sensing the source and focus of his true identity. Notice how the Father interrupts the prayer – because it is being spoken partly out of the new identity ('Father') but partly out of the old ('I am no longer worthy'). The fallacy of the old identity was its notion of being based on his worth, rather than the Father's creative gift of life.

Reflect on, then share together, your own journey to the Father, and so into the new identity that is ours in Christ.

Note the gifts given to affirm his identity:

> The robe, which is the garment of sonship, is accompanied by the ring, which is the insignia of authority and the sandals that distinguish the free man from the slave.
>
> Tom Smail, *The Forgotten Father*

Group exercise: Looking back and looking forward

Share what you have learned.

Share who and what you have valued.

Share any ways you feel you have grown through participation in the course.

Share this in the whole group, or in pairs/triplets.

Identify specific actions you want to:

- *continue from the course;*

- *initiate as a result of the course.*

Share this in pairs/triplets.

Prayer together

As previously, include the prayer of affirmation of the image of God, and allow good space for thanksgiving and affirmations expressed by the group.

Pray for each other in the group.

One way to do this would be for the person who is being prayed for to sit on a chair while others stand 'laying hands' on their shoulder. Pray – with the emphasis on affirmation rather than asking.

Pray that something of Christ's character, strength and grace may grow in this person.

Summary and example timings

	mins
Welcome and opening prayer	5
Reporting back	10
Input and discussion: Freedom from self-concern	20
Bible study and discussion: From the old to the new	20
Group exercise: Looking back and looking forward	20
Prayer together	10

Living beyond the search for identity

Reporting back

Share how your 'action plan' worked out:

■ *successes and failures;*

■ *changes in your own self-understanding and acceptance;*

■ *ways in which others have commented.*

Also, share any ways in which you have been able to give what you have received to others.

Input and discussion: Freedom from self-concern

Many people are searching for their identity in different ways.

Too often the result of that search for identity is becoming obsessed with yourself.

The Bible teaches us that we find our identity when we seek the good of others.
Especially we become free from self-concern and find ourselves in four ways:

Identity in belonging
We find our identity in being part of the body of Christ, the Church – an instrument in an orchestra, not a complete sound in ourselves.

Identity in listening
Our identity takes shape and grows as we listen to God and act in response to his call upon us. This is what it means to follow Jesus and be part of the Church, the called people of God.

Identity in living
God has given us 'richly ... everything for our enjoyment' (1 Timothy 6.17). Jesus came that we might have life in all its fullness (John 10.10). Life involves the enjoyment of creation, social life and the full range of human culture.

Identity in loving
We find our identity when we forget about ourselves and pay attention to God, others and the world.

Bible study and discussion: From the old to the new

Here is another 'exodus' (or Emmaus) journey. The journey into the far country is the journey into a false identity.

> There was a man who had two sons. The younger of them said to his father, 'Father, give me the share of the property that will belong to me.' So he divided his property between them. A few days after the younger son travelled to a distant country, and there he squandered his property in dissolute living. When he had spent everything, a severe famine took place throughout that country, and he began to be in need. So he

went and hired himself to one of the citizens of that country, who sent him to his field to feed the pigs. He would gladly have filled himself with the pods that the pigs were eating; and no one gave him anything. But when he came to himself he said, 'How many of my father's hired hands have bread enough and to spare, but here I am dying of hunger! I will get up and go to my father, and I will say to him, "Father, I have sinned against heaven and before you; I am no longer worthy to be called your son; treat me like one of your hired hands."' So he set off and went to his father. But while he was still far off, his father saw him and was filled with compassion; he ran and put his arms around him and kissed him. Then the son said to him, 'Father, I have sinned against heaven and before you; I am no longer worthy to be called your son.' But the father said to his slaves, 'Quickly, bring out a robe – the best one – and put it on him; put a ring on his finger and sandals on his feet. And get the fatted calf and kill it, and let us eat and celebrate; for this son of mine was dead and is alive again; he was lost and is found!' And they began to celebrate.

Luke 15.11-24

- *Reflect for a few moments in silence on the story.*

- *Share together your own journey into (or chasing after) the false self.*

- *Reflect on, then share together, your own journey to the Father, and so into the new identity that is ours in Christ.*

Some points to note

For the younger son, coming to his senses involves sensing the source and focus of his true identity. Notice how the Father interrupts the prayer – because it is being spoken partly out of the new identity ('Father') but partly out of the old ('I am no longer worthy'). The fallacy of the old identity was its notion of being based on his worth, rather than the Father's creative gift of life.

Note the gifts given to affirm his identity:

> The robe, which is the garment of sonship, is accompanied by the ring, which is the insignia of authority and the sandals that distinguish the free man from the slave.
>
> Tom Smail, *The Forgotten Father*

Group exercise: Looking back and looking forward

Take some time to reflect on the whole of this five-part course in threes and then as a whole group:

- *share what you have learned;*

- *who and what you have valued;*

- *any ways you feel you have grown through participation in the course.*

Identify specific actions you want to:

- *continue from the course;*

- *initiate as a result of the course.*

Prayer together

Pray for each other in the group. The person who is being prayed for sits on a chair, the others stand 'laying hands' on the shoulder. Pray – with the emphasis on affirmation rather than asking – for the writing of the new name on the heart.

Pray the name of Christ also into each person, as all who are baptized into Christ have 'put on Christ'. Pray that something of his character, strength and grace may grow in this person.

Almighty God
we thank you for strengthening us
through our sharing in your Son Jesus Christ.
Through him we offer you our souls and bodies
to be a living sacrifice.
Send us out
in the power of your Spirit
to live and work
to your praise and glory.
Amen.

    Adapted from *Common Worship*: Prayer after Communion, p.182

Living beyond the search for identity

Introduction

Our starting point, in Session One, was the modern search for identity. In it we considered some of the ways in which that search goes off in the wrong direction. Perhaps the deepest mark of fallenness of that search is that its goal is the self. The world, God (however understood) and others are seen as part of the support structure for that self-authentication. But that is to turn truth on its head, for healthy self-acceptance liberates from self-concern.

> 'Friend', said the Spirit, 'could you, only for one moment,
> fix your mind on something not yourself?'
>
> C. S. Lewis, *The Great Divorce*

> Radical faith in Christ frees the Christian from spiritual self-concern to give attention to God and others.
>
> Richard Lovelace, *Dynamics of Spiritual Life*

Scripture teaches by precept and by the lives of those recorded in it, that identity is found when we are not looking for identity itself but life and for the good of others and all creation. Four particular strands form the biblical witness to the fact that identity is found when we are not looking for it, but living the life that God, in Christ, has made possible.

Identity in belonging

Our identity is not a vacuum-packed sealed unit. Rather it is an instrument in an orchestra: one distinct sound blended to make music in the company of others. So easily our modern eyes misread Scripture at this point. When Paul says that he is in travail 'until Christ is formed in you' (Galatians 4.19), he is not so much addressing the individuals in the Church as he is the Church as a whole. 'We are the body of Christ.' Equally, when Peter speaks about the priesthood of all believers, he is not thinking so much of the priesthood of each believer as of the priesthood of the community of faith.

The history of two important modern words illustrates this point. Originally the word individual meant not the isolated self but the community. To say we are individual meant 'we are indivisible', 'we are one'. Our identity is a community identity, modelled after the Trinity. The word identity, in its original use, meant 'we are identical', 'we are one', 'we belong together'. We are more likely to 'find ourselves' as we participate in community than we are by self-analysis; though there needs to be a rhythm between being 'together' and being 'alone'.

Identity in listening

Adam and Eve before the Fall, and Jesus throughout his life, model for us a life that consists of listening to God in the whole of life and choosing the response that expresses his will and character. So Jesus tells the tempter, 'One does not live by bread alone, but by every word that comes from the mouth of God' (Matthew 4.4).

> We are what we hear from God.
>
> Emil Brunner, *The Divine Imperative*

Our identity takes shape and grows as we listen to God, and to the whole of life, and act in response to his call upon us. The very word 'church' (ecclesia) means 'the called out ones', those who have heard God address them and are actively responding to that address. Adam lost his identity at just this point – by not choosing to act upon the word that was calling him into life.

So for us, it is as we listen to God and choose his will that our identity forms and grows.

Identity in living

God has given us richly 'everything for our enjoyment'. By his doing so we are 'enjoined-to' and enriched by all that is. Life involves the enjoyment of creation, social life, and the full range of human culture from the artistic to the athletic. Once we have been liberated from addiction to any aspect of life as the source of our identity, they can become channels through which we are enlarged. So Paul tells us to set our minds on 'whatever is true, whatever is honourable, whatever is just, whatever is pure, whatever is pleasing, whatever is commendable' (Philippians 4.8).

> To love the good, the beautiful, the just, the true is mysteriously to be drawn up into them – or to use another image, to become incarnate of them, to participate in them.
>
> Leanne Payne, *The Healing Presence*

Identity in loving

Our identity is both found, and flourishes best, when we forget ourselves and pay attention to the world, God and others and live within the framework of the two great commandments. The first is this: 'Hear, O Israel, the Lord our God is the only Lord. You shall love the Lord your God with all your heart, with all your soul, with all your mind, and with all your strength.' The second is this: 'Love your neighbour as yourself.' It is in giving that we receive, in loving that we become most fully ourselves. This 'outer-directedness' both blesses others and also heals us of the modern disease of introspection.

Agnes Sanford, the source of so much of the modern healing ministry of the Church, began – after a nervous breakdown – to handle the soil and tend her garden. Gradually she learned to tend people too. It was in giving care and attention to creation and to others that she entered into a most striking and attractive wholeness. That is the path God invites us all to walk.

Called into life

Introduction

This course explores the theme of vocation: the birthright of all the baptized.

The course is built on the foundation principle that human beings are not complete in themselves, but rather beings-in-relationship, who discover their true selves in response to God's call upon their lives. That call is understood to embrace the whole of life, and how we handle relationships, possessions, conflicts, opportunities and suffering. The wellspring of vocation is baptism, which can be described as 'the ordination of the laity', and is best seen as a vocation in itself.

The aim of the course is to develop this sense of vocation from God in the whole of life of every member of the group.

The leaders should, therefore, keeps their eyes on the development and sharpening of each person's sense of vocation in the broadest sense.

The course aims to send people out with a stronger sense of:

- *being called by God in the whole of life (not just in the churchy or spiritual realm);*

- *becoming more fully human through relationship with God;*

- *being part of a 'community that is both called and sent';*

- *being called to share in God's mission in the world.*

The outline of the sessions is as follows:

Session 1: Called by God – open to God's presence

God makes himself known to us in the whole of life. Our task is to learn to recognize him and then act on his word to us. Rather than be 'driven people' we are to live out of a quiet sense of God's call on our lives.

Session 2: Called to conversion – seeing conversion as a way of life

God's call is to change, turn around, repent; not just once, but as a way of life. Christians are called to a distinctive lifestyle. We are to live by the values of the age to come.

Session 3: Called into community – rooted in a faith community

God's call to us makes us Church, the community that is following Christ into life: his body, the expression of his life on earth. Conversion to Christ is vocation to community.

Session 4: Called into mission – participating in the renewal of all creation

Through baptism, every believer is ordained into Christ's mission to bring all creation into life-giving relationship to him.

Health warning

Too easily the Church makes people feel that they ought to listen to God, belong to the Church and be engaged in mission. This course seeks to put all that on the basis of grace. The goal is not to make people do things, or make them guilty about not doing things, but to help them to be in touch with God's call on their lives, so that they live life out of a sense of vocation to love and be loved, listen, belong and participate in God's mission. It is a very different dynamic and motivation.

Note: It is helpful for the leader to read the above each time before the preparation of the next session.

Session One: Called by God

	mins
Opening prayer	10
Introducing vocation	5
Input and discussion: Meeting God at every turn	15
Sharing together	15
Bible study: One particular encounter – Luke 5.1-11	20
Putting it into practice	5
Meditation	10

Session Two: Called to conversion

	mins
Opening prayer	10
Action replay	20
Input and discussion: Conversion – a way of life	15
Bible study: One particular turning-point – Luke 24.28-35	20
Sharing together: My own journey of faith	10
Putting it into practice	5
Meditation	10

Session Three: Called into community

	mins
Opening prayer	5
Action replay	10
Input and discussion: The Church as a community	5
Sharing together	15
Bible study: One particular community – Luke 24.33-49	30
Meditation	15
Putting it into practice	5

Session Four: Called into mission

	mins
Opening prayer	5
Action replay	15
Input and discussion: God's mission to his world	5
Bible study: One particular call to mission – Isaiah 6.1-8	25
Putting it into practice	20
Prayer together	15

Called by God

Opening prayer

Pick up the theme of being called to know God, making use of:

■   *a verse or two from Scripture (e.g. Psalm 46.10-11);*

■   *the words of a song or hymn, said or sung (if said, use one verse only);*

■   *some silence or music to quieten people down from the busyness of the day.*

Introducing vocation

The particular focus of this module is on the nature of our Christian calling or vocation.

'Vocation' is not often spoken of today.

■   *When spoken of, 'vocation' usually refers simply to work.*

■   *Often that work is only what some people do, e.g. doctors, nurses, teachers, clergy.*

■   *Yet being a disciple means being called.*

■   *The Greek word for church, ecclesia, from which we get words like 'ecclesiastical', means 'the called out ones'.*

■   *The Church is the community that has heard God's call and responded to it and continues to be the Church by listening to God's call in the present.*

What that means to each of us, personally, as a group, and as part of the local and universal Church, is what we will be exploring together.

Input and discussion: Meeting God at every turn

This session focuses on how God makes himself known to us today, as he did to the disciples on the way to Emmaus. The aim is to help people develop their awareness of the many different ways this happens.

The Bible is full of stories of people meeting God:

■   *Adam and Eve in the Garden;*

■   *Jacob, on the end of a ladder and in a wrestling match;*

■   *Moses and a burning bush;*

■   *Isaiah in the Temple;*

■   *Zacchaeus up a tree;*

■   *Paul on (or, rather, off) a horse . . .*

We too can expect to experience God as we go through life, but we are more likely to do so if we are looking out for signs of his presence and if we are developing our skills in listening to him. Every experience can become a means by which God communicates with us.

We can experience God:

- *as we enjoy a beautiful part of creation;*

- *as we look at some work of human art or achievement;*

- *through relationship with another person, or an event;*

- *when we come face to face with suffering, evil, or pain (see Terry Waite's story of meeting God in solitary confinement, in his book* Taken on Trust*);*

- *when we are confused by life (St Augustine, sitting in a garden, heard the words 'take and read', which prompted his study of Scripture and his journey into faith – see his famous* Confessions*);*

- *in the daily routines of life (C. S. Lewis was surprised by joy on a London double-decker bus);*

- *in moments of quiet reflection.*

We all have stories to tell of meeting God at surprising moments.

Use some of these examples as a basis for helping the group to get in touch with their experience of God.

Sharing together

This can be done as a whole group, in smaller groups, or pairs.

- *What was your earliest experience of God?*

- *What was your most recent experience of God?*

If there is time (but only after addressing the above questions) you can go on to ask:

- *What has been the most life-changing experience of God you have had?*

In the process of telling their stories, it is good to draw out from people the lessons about how God does make himself known, and how we can help or hinder that communication.

Bible study: One particular encounter – Luke 5.1-11

Jesus came alongside Peter and these disciples and led them to a learning point. There are different ways of describing this – a moment of disclosure, an encounter with God, a revelation. Whatever words we use, what is happening is that God is breaking into someone's life. It usually happens at a surprising moment.

Split the group in two and draw out people's engagement with the story by getting them to look at the following questions:

- *What strikes you most about this story?*

- *In what different ways did Jesus show himself to Peter and these disciples?*

- *How does this connect with our experience?*

- *How, in recent years, has God made himself known to us?*

Putting it into practice

Decide as a group how to act on the insights gained from the Bible study. It is good for the group to come up with its own action plan. However, to get things started, it may be helpful to suggest that in the coming week we:

- *watch out for what God may be saying to us in puzzling/testing situations;*

- *reflect each night on any way in which God has been present to us that day;*

- *be aware of times when God is calling us to be alongside others to point them to God's presence in their experience of life.*

Encourage people to write down what they are going to do. This can either be a group action plan, or individual action plans. Remind people to come next week ready to share joys and struggles in doing what has been agreed.

Meditation

1   Use a symbol of God's revelation of himself to humanity (e.g. a cross, an open Bible, an icon, a candle, etc.) to focus attention on the God who delights to reveal himself.

2   Then, in order to help the group look out beyond its own life, identify some puzzling, tragic, happening that has filled the news this week.

3   Read (or rather, have read) Psalm 46. Perhaps have some quiet music in the background?

4   Give thanks to God for being with us. This can be done in silence.

5   If it is appropriate for the group, sing a song.

6   Join together in a prayer (such as the Collect on the members' handout).

Summary and example timings

	mins
Opening prayer	10
Introducing vocation	5
Input and discussion: Meeting God at every turn	15
Sharing together	15
Bible study: One particular encounter – Luke 5.1-11	20
Putting it into practice	5
Meditation	10

Called by God

Input and discussion: Meeting God at every turn

The Bible is full of stories of people meeting God:

■ *Adam and Eve in the Garden;*

■ *Jacob, on the end of a ladder and in a wrestling match;*

■ *Moses in a burning bush;*

■ *Isaiah in the Temple;*

■ *Zacchaeus up a tree;*

■ *Paul on (or, rather, off) a horse . . .*

We too can expect to experience God as we go through life, but we are more likely to do so if we are looking out for signs of his presence, and if we are developing our skills in listening to him. Every experience can become a means by which God communicates with us.

We can experience God:

■ *as we enjoy a beautiful part of creation;*

■ *as we examine some work of human art or achievement;*

■ *through relationship with another person, or an event;*

■ *when we come face to face with suffering, evil, or pain;*

■ *when we are confused by life;*

■ *in the daily routines of life;*

■ *in moments of quiet reflection.*

We all have stories to tell of meeting God at surprising moments.

Sharing together

■ *What was your earliest experience of God?*

■ *What was your most recent experience of God?*

■ *What has been the most life-changing experience of God you have had?*

Bible study: One particular encounter – Luke 5.1-11

> Once while Jesus was standing beside the lake of Gennesaret, and the crowd was pressing in on him to hear the word of God, he saw two boats there at the shore of the lake; the fishermen had gone out of them and were washing their nets. He got into one of the boats, the one belonging to Simon, and asked him to put out a little way from the shore. Then he sat down and taught the crowds from the boat. When he had finished speaking, he said to Simon, 'Put out into the deep water and let down your nets for a catch.' Simon answered, 'Master, we have worked all night long but have caught nothing. Yet if you say so, I will let down the nets.' When they had done this, they caught so many fish that their nets were beginning to break. So they signalled their partners in the other boat to come and help them. And they came and filled both boats, so that they began to sink. But when Simon Peter saw it, he fell down at Jesus' knees, saying, 'Go away from me, Lord, for I am a sinful man!' For he and all who were with him were amazed at the catch of fish that they had taken; and so also were James and John, sons of Zebedee, who were partners with Simon. Then Jesus said to Simon, 'Do not be afraid; from now on you will be catching people.' When they had brought their boats to shore, they left everything and followed him.

- *What strikes you most about this story?*

- *In what different ways did Jesus show himself to Peter and these disciples?*

- *How does this connect with our experience?*

Putting it into practice

Decide how to act on the insights gained from the Bible study.

Come to the next session ready to share the joys and struggles in trying to do what has been agreed.

Meditation

God speaks to humanity as a whole, to society and to churches, as well as individuals.

This meditation focuses on the ways that God is speaking to our world today.

> God is our refuge and strength,
> a very present help in trouble.
> Therefore we will not fear, though the earth should change,
> though the mountains shake in the heart of the sea;
> though its waters roar and foam,
> though the mountains tremble with its tumult.
>
> There is a river whose streams make glad the city of God,
> the holy habitation of the Most High.
> God is in the midst of the city; it shall not be moved;
> God will help it when the morning dawns.

The nations are in an uproar, the kingdoms totter;
he utters his voice, the earth melts.
The Lord of hosts is with us;
the God of Jacob is our refuge.

Come, behold the works of the Lord;
see what desolations he has brought on the earth.
He makes wars cease to the end of the earth;
he breaks the bow, and shatters the spear;
he burns the shield with fire.
'Be still, and know that I am God!
I am exalted among the nations,
I am exalted in the earth.'
The Lord of hosts is with us;
the God of Jacob is our refuge.

Psalm 46

Almighty Father,
who in your great mercy gladdened the disciples
with the sight of the risen Lord:
give us such knowledge of his presence with us,
that we may be strengthened and sustained by his risen life
and serve you continually in righteousness and truth;
through Jesus Christ your Son our Lord,
who is alive and reigns with you,
in the unity of the Holy Spirit,
one God, now and for ever. Amen.

Common Worship: Collect for the Third Sunday of Easter

Something to think over

The Christian should be a called, not a driven, person; someone able to be still and wait to hear God's voice, not rushing around fulfilling everybody else's expectation of them.

Called to conversion

Opening prayer

Pick up the theme of God's call to conversion/change making use of:

- *a verse or two from Scripture (e.g. Psalm 40.1-3);*

- *the words of a song/hymn, said or sung (if said use one verse only);*

- *some silence/music to quieten people down from the busyness of the day.*

Action replay

Either in small groups or all together, remind people about your 'Putting it into practice' plans agreed at the end of the last session. Invite people to share successes or struggles in doing this.

Input and discussion: Conversion – a way of life

Introduce the subject by drawing on the following (or your own) material.

The popular understanding of conversion, both inside and outside the Church, is at fault on two counts.

First, conversion is thought of as a once in a lifetime event – such as a car being converted to run on gas. But, like the car, conversion leads to a way of life. It is an attitude of orientation towards God that affects every day and every aspect of life. The Greek word is *metanoia*: it means a whole change of mind and outlook. It involves turning round (repentance). It is at the heart of all true learning – seeing life from a new perspective and changing our behaviour accordingly.

Second, conversion is thought of as simply a religious/spiritual experience, whereas it is essentially about a way of life. In the monastic tradition the three vows of 'poverty, chastity and obedience' actually form just one vow. It is a vow of conversion – commitment to a changed lifestyle based on a new way of seeing reality.

This is what Christian baptism involves: commitment to a life of openness to turning, repentance, change, conversion.

Ask the group how they respond to this idea. Does it make sense? Does it leave them with any questions? There is no need to have a long discussion at this point. All that is needed is to ensure that people are with you.

Bible study: One particular turning-point – Luke 24.28-35

Before you begin to look at the passage prepare everyone for the exercise b
y setting the scene. Imagine what those two disciples, as they started out the
journey, thought would lie ahead that evening and over the days to come. Paint as
vivid a picture as you can.

Read the passage and give some moments for quiet thought or discussion in pairs.

Then invite the group to say how – one year on – those disciples would have seen life. What would be the immediate and long-term consequences of such an experience?

Get into this discussion by asking questions like:

■ *What would have been good news for them better than they could ever have imagined?*

■ *What would have been the major changes in their lives?*

■ *What would it have cost them?*

With these and other questions that come to you, help the group to explore what conversion – turning life around in the direction of Jesus – meant for these two disciples.

Move on to explore the impact of our faith on our experience of life.

Are there similar things you can point to in your faith journey?

Sharing together: My own journey of faith

In smaller groups ask these questions. Since we began the journey of faith:

■ *What has been the good news about our experience of faith in Christ?*

■ *What have been the major changes in our lives?*

■ *What has it cost us?*

■ *How can our lives be marked by openness, availability and obedience to God?*

You may want people to address this last question individually. Invite people to reflect in silence about this one. They may wish to write something down; draw a picture; or just sit quietly.

If there is time, thoughts could be shared with a neighbour. But this is optional.

Putting it into practice

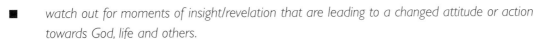

Decide as a group how to act on the insights gained from this session.

It is good for the group to come up with its own action plan. However, to get things started it may be helpful to suggest that in the coming days we:

■ *watch out for moments of insight/revelation that are leading to a changed attitude or action towards God, life and others.*

Come to the next session ready to share the joys and struggles in trying to do what has been agreed.

You may like to think about this. Someone once said: 'If you were up in court next week accused of being a Christian, would there be enough evidence to convict you?'

Encourage people to write down what they are going to do. This can either be a group action plan, or individual action plans. Remind people to come next week ready to share their experience of trying to do what has been agreed.

Meditation

Possible introduction

The twelve-step programme of Alcoholics Anonymous (developed by two Christians) is a striking example of a model of conversion as a way of life. In a real sense the Christian Church can be described as 'sinners anonymous', a group of people taking responsibility for fundamental change in their lives, with the help of a 'Higher Power' and the company of others making that journey.

1   Again, use a symbol of God's revelation of himself to humanity (e.g. a cross, an open Bible, an icon, a candle, etc.) to focus attention on the God who calls us to know him.

2   Read (or rather, have read) Ephesians 4.17-25; 5.1-2, which is printed on the members' handout. Again, you may wish to have quiet music in the background.

3   Invite people to respond in prayer to the passage and to what we have learned/experienced during the time together in this session. Encourage this to be done either in silence, or aloud (as appropriate for the group), or both.

4   If it is appropriate for your group, sing a song.

5   Join together in a prayer (such as the Prayer of Preparation, printed on the members' handout).

Summary and example timings

	mins
Opening prayer	10
Action replay	20
Input and discussion: Conversion – a way of life	15
Bible study: One particular turning-point – Luke 24.28-35	20
Sharing together: My own journey of faith	10
Putting it into practice	5
Meditation	10

Called to conversion

Input and discussion: Conversion – a way of life

> Few Christians are ever fully evangelised.
> All our lives we need the power of the gospel to transform us.
>
> *The Rite of Christian Initiation of Adults*

The popular understanding of conversion is at fault on two counts.

First, conversion is thought of as a once in a lifetime event. The Greek word is *metanoia*, which means a whole change of mind and outlook and a turning round (repentance).

Secondly, conversion is thought of as simply a religious/spiritual experience, whereas it is essentially about a way of life – commitment to a changed lifestyle based on a new way of seeing reality.

This is what Christian baptism involves: commitment to a life of openness to turning, repentance, change, conversion.

Bible study: One particular turning-point –
Luke 24.28-35

> As they came near the village to which they were going, he walked ahead as
> if he were going on. But they urged him strongly, saying, 'Stay with us, because it is almost
> evening and the day is now nearly over.' So he went in to stay with them. When he was
> at the table with them, he took bread, blessed and broke it, and gave it to them. Then
> their eyes were opened, and they recognized him; and he vanished from their sight. They
> said to each other, 'Were not our hearts burning within us while he was talking to us on
> the road, while he was opening the scriptures to us?' That same hour they got up and
> returned to Jerusalem; and they found the eleven and their companions gathered
> together. They were saying, 'The Lord has risen indeed, and he has appeared to Simon!'
> Then they told what had happened on the road, and how he had been made known
> to them in the breaking of the bread.
>
> Luke 24.28-35

Sharing together: My own journey of faith

Since we began the journey of faith:

- *What has been the good news about our experience of faith in Christ?*

- *What have been the major changes in our lives?*

- *What has it cost us?*

- *How can our lives be marked by openness, availability and obedience to God?*

Putting it into practice

Decide how to act on the insights gained from this session.

Meditation

The twelve-step programme of Alcoholics Anonymous (developed by two Christians) is a striking example of a model of conversion as a way of life. In a real sense the Christian Church can be described as 'sinners anonymous', a group of people taking responsibility for fundamental change in their lives, with the help of a 'Higher Power' and the company of others making that journey.

Now this I affirm and insist on in the Lord: you must no longer live as the Gentiles live, in the futility of their minds. They are darkened in their understanding, alienated from the life of God because of their ignorance and hardness of heart. They have lost all sensitivity and have abandoned themselves to licentiousness, greedy to practise every kind of impurity. That is not the way you learned Christ! For surely you have heard about him and were taught in him, as truth is in Jesus. You were taught to put away your former way of life, your old self, corrupt and deluded by its lusts, and to be renewed in the spirit of your minds, and to clothe yourselves with the new self, created according to the likeness of God in true righteousness and holiness.

So then putting away falsehood, let all of us speak the truth to our neighbours ... Therefore be imitators of God, as beloved children, and live in love, as Christ loved us and gave himself up for us, a fragrant offering and sacrifice to God.

Ephesians 4.17-25, 5.1-2

Almighty God,
to whom all hearts are open,
all desires known,
and from whom no secrets are hidden:
cleanse the thoughts of our hearts
by the inspiration of your Holy Spirit,
that we may perfectly love you,
and worthily magnify your holy name;
through Christ our Lord. Amen.

Common Worship: Prayer of Preparation

True and perfect wisdom consists in departing from evil and doing good.

St Bernard of Clairvaux (on the Song of Songs)

Something to ponder

Spirituality is increasingly popular today. It is about how we encounter God. It is about the transcendent dimension in life. It is about how we make sense of life. However, there are two aspects of conversion that are vital marks of a healthy spirituality.

One is that Christian spirituality is a transformative experience. It is intended to be, and is authenticated by, transformation in a person's life. Much popular 'spirituality' is about staying as I am and feeding my ideas and preferences; whereas Christian spirituality leads us to be changed – by love.

The other is that Christian spirituality is about being yielded, or available, to God, just as Jesus was. Yet, in much modern spirituality, various practices are engaged in so that we can have better 'control' over our lives. Jesus has shown us that fullness of humanity involves a yielded availability to God.

> One does not live by bread alone, but by every word that comes
> from the mouth of God.
>
> Matthew 4.3

Christian spirituality is, therefore, essentially a way of approaching life shaped by openness, availability and obedience to God. This transforms who we are, how we see life, and how we live life. Conversion is our way of life, resourced by faith.

Called into community

In this session more time is given to the meditation at the end, which includes space for free or open prayer. The action plan in 'putting it into practice' then happens after the prayer, thus reversing the normal order of the other sessions.

Opening prayer

Pick up the theme of God's call to mission, making use of:

■   *a verse or two from Scripture (e.g. John 13.34-35);*

■   *the words of a song/hymn, said or sung (if said use one verse only);*

■   *some silence or music to quieten people down from the busyness of the day.*

Action replay

Either in small groups or all together, remind people of what was agreed at the end of the last session. Refer to the action plans that were written.

Once again, invite people to share successes/struggles in doing this. As in each session, be open to people having something to share that does not fit your questions. Welcome such contributions, but do not be led off course.

Input and discussion: The Church as a community

Points to draw on:

■   *The Church is a community rather than an organization.*

It has organization, but it is a community. Organizations have a specific purpose, and people within them have clearly defined roles, which they fulfil (or fail to fulfil). Organizations usually have a clear hierarchy of importance and rewards. In a good organization, relationships are important, but the primary goal is 'getting the job done'.

A community has its focus more on being than doing. People are there primarily for who they are rather than what they do. Honour is given to the weakest members – as in a family with young children or a handicapped person. Relationships are what community is largely about. The way that Christ has established his Church is that it is a community and has an organization. It is also a community that has a task beyond itself – participating in his mission in the world.

■   *The experience of a life-giving community is a gift in two ways.*

1   It is God's gift to the Church and all human society. Community belongs to the very nature of God. God is Holy Trinity – three-in-one. God is Being-in-communion/community. We reflect his image because we are social beings. Community is possible through the gifts of truth, forgiveness and the presence of Christ.

2　It is the Church's gift to the world. Our world today is suffering a breakdown and loss of community. High mobility, the emphasis on 'doing your own thing', pressurized working life and the breakdown of families all contribute to this. One of the greatest gifts the Church can give the world today is the experience of a working community – one that is good news for those in it, and those beyond it.

Does this make sense to you?

We all have good and bad experiences of community and organizations. Even small groups can have problems and become stuck:

> Groups are very good at developing little rituals of dishonesty, ways of systematically evading real issues.
>
> Simon Tugwell, *Did You Receive the Spirit?*

Jesus clearly had problems in his group! However, issues were addressed, and costly forgiveness became a way of life for all.

Sharing together

Share with each other, together or in small groups, your best and worst experiences of communities and organizations.

Bible study: One particular community – Luke 24.33-49

When these disciples turned round the first thing they did was to go back to their fellow disciples. In the verses for this session we see the Church being formed.

We are now going beyond the customary end of the Emmaus road story to see how the risen Christ instructs and encourages his disciples.

What follows is an exercise to help us get in touch with the roots of the Christian community. There are two ideas here (you may do one or both).

1　Reporting

Imagine you arrived on the scene just before verse 33, and left immediately after verse 49. You have a friend who heard you were there, or have been contacted by a reporter from a local newspaper, who is asking you to explain what was going on, what was it like? How would you report this experience – without using any churchy words like 'fellowship', 'ministry', 'testimony', etc.?

2　Mapping

Think of this community as a compass with Jesus in the centre. How would we label the four points of this compass that give the best description we can think of? Read the passage and try to understand what was going on. Avoid churchy words and identify the four major characteristics of the group in everyday language.

It is good for us to be reminded of what 'church' is all about, and to see the things that are essential to its life. Either choose one of the exercises for everyone to work on or divide the group in two and do one exercise each. If you do this, allow time for the groups to report back. You can, of course, work in smaller groups even if you do only one exercise. Having done this exercise, help the group to consider the application of what has emerged, by asking questions such as:

- *How can we as a group be the sort of community of faith we have been looking at?*

- *What part can we play in enabling our local church to be more like the Church we have been studying?*

Meditation

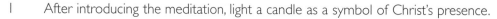

Before starting the meditation, explain that, after the reading, there will be space to respond to the prayer that is printed in the members' handout. This could be silent prayer, but here is a particularly good opportunity for a group to pray out loud together. Where groups are not familiar with praying like that, suggest that they pick up a phrase from the prayer of Paul's, and either add their own request such as 'help us to be like that', or to leave some silence and then use the sentence and response: *Lord, in your mercy: Hear our prayer.*

1   After introducing the meditation, light a candle as a symbol of Christ's presence.

2   In silence or out loud give thanks to God for being with us.

3   If it is appropriate for your group, sing a song.

4   Read (or rather, have read) Ephesians 3.14-19 (on the members' handouts).

5   Invite people, as previously directed, to respond in prayer, and then close with these words:

> Now to him who by the power at work within us is able to accomplish abundantly far more than all we can ask or imagine, to him be glory in the church and in Christ Jesus to all generations, for ever and ever. Amen.
>
> Ephesians 3.20-21

Putting it into practice

The real problem we have with the Church as a community is not about understanding it, but practising it.

Decide as a group how to act on the insights gained from this session. As with previous sessions, it is good for the group to come up with its own action plan. However, to get things started it may be helpful to suggest that in the coming week we:

- *commit ourselves to act in some specific way to contribute to the community life of this group/church;*

In which case we need to come ready next week to answer:

- *What steps have I taken to help build community wherever I go?*

- *What opportunities have I had to build community in the Church?*

However, the group may well want to identify some specific action it wants to take, such as speaking to newcomers at church, meeting to pray with each other, or in some other way to take a specific piece of action.

Encourage people to write down what they are going to do. This can either be a group action plan, or individual action plans. Remind people to come next week ready to share joys and struggles in doing what has been agreed.

Summary and example timings

	mins
Opening prayer	5
Action replay	10
Input and discussion: The Church as a community	5
Sharing together	15
Bible study: One particular community – Luke 24.33-49	30
Meditation	15
Putting it into practice	5

Called into community

Input and discussion: The Church as a community

The gift of community

The experience of a life-giving community is a gift in two ways. It is God's gift to the Church and all human society, which arises out of the fact that community belongs to the very nature of God. God is three-in-one, a Being-in-communion/ community. We can reflect his image because he has given us of himself by making us in his image as social beings. He has also given us the gifts of truth and forgiveness and the presence of Christ to make it possible.

The other way in which community is to be a gift is from the Church to the world around us. The world today is suffering a breakdown and loss of community. High mobility, the emphasis on 'doing your own thing', pressurized working life and the breakdown of families all contribute. One of the greatest gifts the Church can give the world today is the experience of a working community — one that is good news for those in it, and those beyond it.

Sharing together

Share with each other, together or in small groups, your best and worst experiences of communities and organizations.

Bible study: One particular community — Luke 24. 33-49

When the disciples return to Jerusalem, they become involved in the forming of a church. It is good to be reminded of what church, in the first place, was all about.

> That same hour they got up and returned to Jerusalem; and they found the eleven and their companions gathered together. They were saying, 'The Lord has risen indeed, and he has appeared to Simon!' Then they told what had happened on the road, and how he had been made known to them in the breaking of the bread.
>
> While they were talking about this, Jesus himself stood among them and said to them, 'Peace be with you.' They were startled and terrified, and thought that they were seeing a ghost. He said to them, 'Why are you frightened, and why do doubts arise in your hearts? Look at my hands and my feet; see that it is I myself. Touch me and see; for a ghost does not have flesh and bones as you see that I have.' And when he had said this, he showed them his hands and his feet. While in their joy they were disbelieving and still wondering, he said to them, 'Have you anything here to eat?' They gave him a piece of broiled fish, and he took it and ate in their presence.
>
> Then he said to them, 'These are my words that I spoke to you while I was still with you — that everything written about me in the law of Moses, the prophets, and the psalms

must be fulfilled.' Then he opened their minds to understand the scriptures, and he said to them, 'Thus it is written, that the Messiah is to suffer and to rise from the dead on the third day, and that repentance and forgiveness of sins is to be proclaimed in his name to all nations, beginning from Jerusalem. You are witnesses of these things. And see, I am sending upon you what my Father promised; so stay here in the city until you have been clothed with power from on high.'

Luke 24.33-49

Meditation

For this reason I bow my knees before the Father, from whom every family in heaven and on earth takes its name. I pray that, according to the riches of his glory, he may grant that you may be strengthened in your inner being with power through his Spirit, and that Christ may dwell in your hearts through faith, as you are being rooted and grounded in love. I pray that you may have the power to comprehend, with all the saints, what is the breadth and length and height and depth, and to know the love of Christ that surpasses knowledge, so that you may be filled with all the fullness of God.

Now to him who by the power at work within us is able to accomplish abundantly far more than all we can ask or imagine, to him be glory in the church and in Christ Jesus to all generations, forever and ever. Amen.

Ephesians 3.14-20

Putting it into practice

Decide how to act on the insights gained from this session.

Come to the next session ready to share the joys and struggles in trying to do what has been agreed.

Closing thought

The Church will never discover what it means to lay down its life for the world until its members begin to lay down their lives for one another.

Jim Wallis, *The Call to Conversion*

Called into mission

Opening prayer

Pick up the theme of God's call to mission, making use of:

- *a verse or two from Scripture (e.g. Isaiah 42.6-7);*

- *the words of a song/hymn, said or sung;*

- *some silence/music to quieten people down from the busyness of the day.*

Action replay

Either in small groups or all together, remind people of what was agreed at the end of the last session. Refer to the 'Putting it into practice' plans.

Invite people to share successes/struggles in doing this as in previous weeks.

Input and discussion: God's mission to his world

Make use of the following points, or develop your own introduction.

- *Mission is first and foremost what God does in sending Jesus and the Holy Spirit to forward his work of gathering up all creation into his purposes of love from which it has fallen.*

- *'Our' mission is nothing other than to join in with what God is doing. So even Jesus said: 'Very truly, I tell you, the Son can do nothing on his own, but only what he sees the Father doing' (John 5.19).*

- *There is much more to mission than many Christians think. You may like to draw a simple visual aid as you talk through this section. In the centre of a large piece of paper write the words 'God's Mission' with four arrows coming out to the four points of the compass. By each arrow write the words: 'Heals, Confronts, Overcomes, Proclaims'.*

1 God's mission heals

It is God's mission to gather up all creation into his purposes, bringing peace, harmony and right relationship to him of all that exists. It includes the environment and human society, issues of justice and peace, and right relationship between groups of people and in communities (including families). God's mission is at work in all these areas bringing healing where things are damaged, broken or 'out of joint'.

2 God's mission confronts

As we see in Jesus' relationship to religious leaders, it will often involve us in confronting wrong, though often this is by doing right rather than preaching at others.

3 God's mission overcomes

In confronting wrong it is all too easy to use the weapons of this world to establish God's kingdom, but that is not Christ's way, which is one of overcoming evil with good (see Course

Two, 'Overcoming evil'), speaking the truth in love, and making sacrifices for the good of those most in need.

When we are baptized we are commissioned to participate in this mission. We are called to be 'faithful soldiers and servants of Christ to our lives' end'.

4   God's mission proclaims

The first disciples and the whole Church were commissioned to proclaim the gospel – the good news – to the whole creation, in words as well as in actions. It is through the preaching of the good news in words that individual people are stirred to faith and themselves called to join in God's mission (Romans 10.14).

Bible study: One particular call to mission – Isaiah 6.1-8

There are two aspects of any call to share in God's mission:

- *the task to be done and*

- *the grace/resources to do it.*

Together or in two groups consider:

- *What was the task Isaiah was given?*

- *What resources were made available to him?*

For both of these questions also consider:

- *What is our task today?*

- *What resources does God make available to us?*

Get the groups to report their findings to each other.

Putting it into practice

Take the time to share with one another:

- *what you have discovered about the shape of your own calling during this whole module;*

- *what this is likely to mean in practice for you;*

- *if there is a particular commitment you want to make and share with others.*

Prayer together

Draw on:

- *the patterns from earlier sessions;*

- *the experience of the group, and*

- *the Scripture, Collect and responses on the members' handouts*

to develop a suitable 'commission' focus to this closing act of prayer together.

Summary and example timings

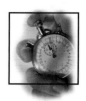

	mins
Opening prayer	5
Action replay	15
Input and discussion: God's mission to his world	5
Bible study: One particular call to mission – Isaiah 6.1-8	25
Putting it into practice	20
Prayer together	15

Called into mission

Action replay

Share the successes and struggles of trying to put into practice what was agreed at the end of the last session.

Input and discussion: God's mission to his world

There is more to mission than many Christians think.

1   God's mission heals

It is God's mission to bring peace, harmony and right relationship to him of all that exists, including the environment and human society, issues of justice and peace, and right relationship between groups of people.

2   God's mission confronts

As in Jesus' relationship to religious leaders, it will often involve us in confronting wrong.

3   God's mission overcomes

In confronting wrong, Christ's way is one of overcoming evil with good. Our baptism commissions us to participate in this mission.

4   God's mission proclaims

It is through the preaching of the good news in words that individual people are stirred to faith and themselves called to join in God's mission (Romans 10.14).

Bible study: One particular call to mission – Isaiah 6.1-8

> In the year that King Uzziah died, I saw the Lord sitting on a throne, high and lofty; and the hem of his robe filled the temple. Seraphs were in attendance above him; each had six wings: with two they covered their faces, and with two they covered their feet, and with two they flew. And one called to another and said:
>
> 'Holy, holy, holy is the Lord of hosts;
> the whole earth is full of his glory.'
>
> The pivots on the thresholds shook at the voices of those who called, and the house filled with smoke. And I said: 'Woe is me! I am lost, for I am a man of unclean lips, and I live among a people of unclean lips; yet my eyes have seen the King, the Lord of hosts!' Then one of the seraphs flew to me, holding a live coal that had been taken from the altar with a pair of tongs. The seraph touched my mouth with it and said: 'Now that this has touched your lips, your guilt has departed and your sin is blotted out.' Then I heard the voice of the Lord saying, 'Whom shall I send, and who will go for us?' And I said, 'Here am I; send me!'
>
> Isaiah 6.1-8

Putting it into practice

- *What have you discovered about the shape of your own calling during this whole module?*

- *What is this likely to mean in practice for you?*

- *Is there a particular commitment you want to make and share with others?*

Meditation

This passage from Paul's letter to the Romans, chapter 8, is one of the great mission passages of the New Testament. It contains the three-fold groan of God's world, as it looks for the coming of his kingdom in the fullness of time.

- *First, is the groaning of creation, damaged by war and pollution and disconnected from God's purpose of blessing to and through it.*

- *Second, is the groaning of the Christian, as we realize that our hopes and longings and desires for God are so easily frustrated and sidetracked by our need to prove ourselves, and please or control others.*

- *Third, is the groaning of the Spirit, as – like Jesus – he weeps over the city of human existence. We touch that grief and pain – and hope – in the heart of God when we pray.*

I consider that the sufferings of this present time are not worth comparing with the glory about to be revealed to us. For the creation waits with eager longing for the revealing of the children of God; for the creation was subjected to futility, not of its own will but by the will of the one who subjected it, in hope that the creation itself will be set free from its bondage to decay and will obtain the freedom of the glory of the children of God. We know that the whole creation has been groaning in labour pains until now; and not only the creation, but we ourselves, who have the first fruits of the Spirit, groan inwardly while we wait for adoption, the redemption of our bodies. For in hope we were saved. Now hope that is seen is not hope. For who hopes for what is seen? But if we hope for what we do not see, we wait for it with patience. Likewise, the Spirit helps us in our weakness; for we do not know how to pray as we ought, but that very Spirit intercedes with sighs too deep for words. And God, who searches the heart, knows what is the mind of the Spirit, because the Spirit intercedes for the saints according to the will of God.

Romans 8.18-27

Collect

Eternal Father,
who at the baptism of Jesus
revealed him to be your Son,
anointing him with the Holy Spirit:
grant to us, who are born again by water and the Spirit,
that we may be faithful to our calling as your adopted children;
through Jesus Christ your Son our Lord,
who is alive and reigns with you,
in the unity of the Holy Spirit,
one God, now and for ever. Amen.

Common Worship: Collect for the First Sunday of Epiphany

Leader:
Lord, send us out
in the power of your Spirit
to live and work
to your praise and glory.
All: Amen.

Leader:
Go in peace to love and serve the Lord.
All: In the name of Christ. Amen.

Closing thought

To engage in mission is to participate in the movement of God's
love towards people, since God is a fountain of sending love.

David Bosch, *Transforming Mission*

Bibliography and further reading

Bibliography

Common Worship, Church House Publishing, 2000.

Common Worship: Daily Prayer, Church House Publishing, 2002.

Roberta Bondi, *To Pray and to Love*, Burns & Oates, 1991.

David Bosch, *Transforming Mission*, Orbis Books, 1992.

Emil Brunner, *The Divine Imperative*, Lutterworth, 1942.

Catholic Church, *Rite of Christian Initiation of Adults*, Geoffrey Chapman, 1987.

T. S. Eliot, *Collected Poems 1909–1962*, Faber & Faber, 1974.

Luke T. Johnson, *Sharing Possessions*, SCM, 1986.

John Kavanaugh, *Following Christ in a Consumer Society – Still*, Orbis Books, 1991.

C. S. Lewis, *The Great Divorce*, Fontana, 1957.

Richard Lovelace, *Dynamics of Spiritual Life*, Paternoster Press, 1979.

Henri Nouwen, *Life of the Beloved*, Hodder & Stoughton, 1992.

Leanne Payne, *The Healing Presence*, Kingsway, 1989.

Gottfried Quell, *Sin*, A & C Black, 1951.

Tom Smail, *The Forgotten Father*, Hodder & Stoughton, 1980.

Paul Tournier, *The Meaning of Persons*, SCM, 1957.

Simon Tugwell, *Did You Receive the Spirit?*, Darton, Longman & Todd, 1979.

Jim Wallis, *The Call to Conversion*, Lion, 1981.

John Westerhoff, *Living the Faith Community*, Harper & Row, 1985.

Further reading

Augustine, *Confessions*, Penguin, 1961.

Richard Foster, *Prayer*, Hodder & Stoughton, 1992.

Nicky Gumbel, *Challenging Lifestyle*, Kingsway, 2000.

Michael Marshall, *Flame in the Mind*, Zondervan, 2003.

Michael Mayne, *Learning to Dance*, Darton, Longman & Todd, 2001.

Scott Peck, *The Road Less Travelled*, Arrow Books, 1983.

John Powell, *Why Am I Afraid to Tell You Who I Am?*, Fontana/Collins, 1969.

Janice Price, *Telling Our Faith Story*, Church House Publishing, 1999.

Terry Waite, *Taken on Trust*, Coronet, 1994.

Robert Warren, *An Affair of the Heart*, Highland Books, 1994.

Philip Yancey, *What's so Amazing about Grace?*, Zondervan, 1997.

The authors

Stephen Cottrell is Canon Pastor at Peterborough Cathedral and an Associate Missioner with Springboard, the Archbishops' initiative for evangelism. Prior to this he was the Wakefield Diocesan Missioner. He is the author of *Catholic Evangelism, Praying Through Life* and, with Steven Croft, *Travelling Well; A Companion Guide to the Christian Faith*.

Steven Croft is Warden of Cranmer Hall within St John's College, Durham. He was previously Vicar of Ovenden in Halifax for nine years and Mission Consultant in the Diocese of Wakefield. He is the author of the handbooks *Growing New Christians* and *Making New Disciples,* and his work has pioneered understanding of the relationship between evangelism and nurture. His recent work includes *Ministry in Three Dimensions: Ordination and Leadership in the Local Church* and *Transforming Communities*.

John Finney is the retired Bishop of Pontefract and former Decade of Evangelism Officer for the Church of England. His research report *Finding Faith Today* has been instrumental in helping the Church understand how people become Christians. He was also involved in the writing of *On the Way – Towards an Integrated Approach to Christian Initiation* for General Synod and is the author of several books on evangelism and renewal.

Felicity Lawson has been Dean of Ministry and Director of Ordinands in the Diocese of Wakefield. Together with John Finney she wrote *Saints Alive!,* a nurture course helping Christians towards a deeper understanding of life in the Spirit. She has recently returned to parish ministry as Vicar of Gildersome, near Leeds.

Robert Warren was Team Rector of one of the largest and fastest growing churches in England, St Thomas, Crookes. In 1993 he succeeded John Finney as the Church of England's National Officer for Evangelism. He is now working full time as a member of the Springboard Team. He is the author of a number of books including *Building Missionary Congregations*, which points to the work of helping people on the journey of faith as one of the key tasks for the Church in the twenty-first century.

Although all five authors are Anglicans, the *Emmaus* material can be used by any denomination and has been produced with this in mind.

Using the CD-ROM

Running the CD-ROM

Windows PC users

The CD-ROM should start automatically. If you need to start the application manually, click on *Start* and select *Run*, then type **d:\lifestyle.exe** (where **d** is the letter of your CD-ROM drive) and click on OK. The menu that appears gives you access to all the resources on the CD. No software is installed on to your computer.

Mac users

Use the Finder to locate the resources in the folders described below. The menu application will not work on a Mac, but you will still be able to access the resources.

Viruses

We have checked the CD-ROM for viruses throughout its creation. However, you are advised to run your own virus-checking software over the CD-ROM before using it. Church House Publishing and The Archbishops' Council accept no responsibility for damage or loss of data on your systems, however caused.

Copyright

The material on the CD-ROM is copyright © The Archbishops' Council 2003, unless otherwise specified. All industry trademarks are acknowledged. You are free to use this material within your own church or group, but the material must not be further distributed in any form without written permission from Church House Publishing. When using images or resources from the CD-ROM please include the appropriate copyright notice.

Handouts

The written resources require *Adobe Acrobat Reader* for display and printing. If *Acrobat Reader* is already installed on your computer, it will be loaded automatically whenever required. If you do not have it, you can install *Acrobat Reader* from the program within the **acrobat** folder on the CD, or by downloading the Reader from www.adobe.com. Please note that Acrobat files cannot be edited.

Error messages

You may receive the error message, 'There is no application associated with the given file name extension.' If you are trying to read one of the handouts, you should install the *Adobe Acrobat Reader* and try again. If you are opening one of the image files, your system does not have any software registered for use with JPEG or TIFF files. Install the free copy of IrfanView and during its installation make sure you associate .TIF and .JPG extensions with IrfanView.

PowerPoint presentation

The CD-ROM contains presentations on *Emmaus* using Microsoft's PowerPoint. This will enable you to present the key facts about the course to groups within your church.

If you have PowerPoint 97 or later installed on your computer, you can use it to run the presentation directly from the CD. The presentations are in named folders within the **ppt** folder on the CD. If you do not have PowerPoint, install the free viewer **PPView97.exe** from the **ppt** folder itself.

If the text in the presentation is poorly displayed, use the version of the presentation called pngsetup.exe. This will copy the presentation to your PC, complete with embedded fonts.

Links

The links to web sites require an active Internet connection. Please ensure you can browse the web before selecting an external web site. We accept no responsibility for the content of sites not produced by Church House Publishing.

Further help

If you experience problems with the CD, please visit the *Emmaus* web site at www.e-mmaus.org.uk. We will post further help or support issues on this site.

Emmaus: The Way of Faith

If you have enjoyed using *Christian Lifestyle*, you may be interested in the other *Emmaus: The Way of Faith* material. This resource is aimed at adults and is designed to help churches welcome people into the Christian faith and the life of the Church. It is rooted in an understanding of evangelism, nurture and discipleship that is modelled on the example of Jesus, as portrayed in the story of the Emmaus road.

Emmaus has three stages: **contact, nurture** and **growth**. It begins by encouraging the vision of the local church for evangelism and giving practical advice on how to develop **contact** with those outside the Church. The course material provided includes a 15-week **nurture** course that covers the basics of the Christian life and four **growth** books, including *Christian Lifestyle*, that offer Christians an opportunity to deepen their understanding of Christian living and discipleship.

Emmaus: The Way of Faith Introduction: 2nd edition
£4.95   0 7151 4963 6
Essential background to both the theology and practice of *Emmaus* and includes material on how to run the course in your own church.

Leading an Emmaus Group
£5.95   0 7151 4905 9
Straightforward and direct guide to leading both Nurture and Growth groups. It lays a biblical framework for group leadership, using Jesus as the example and model.

Contact: 2nd Edition
£5.95   0 7151 4995 4
Explores ways that your church can be involved in evangelism and outreach and make contact with those outside the Church.

Nurture: 2nd Edition
£22.50   0 7151 4994 6
A 15-session course covering the basics of Christian life and faith. (Includes CD-ROM).

Growth: Knowing God
£17.50   0 7151 4875 3
Four short courses for growing Christians: Living the Gospel; Knowing the Father; Knowing Jesus; and Come, Holy Spirit.

Growth: Growing as a Christian
£17.50   0 7151 4876 1
Five short courses for growing Christians: Growing in Prayer; Growing in the Scriptures; Being Church; Growing in Worship; and Life, Death and Christian Hope.

Growth: Christian Lifestyle
£22.50   0 7151 4006 X
Four short courses for growing Christians: Living Images; Overcoming Evil; Personal Identity; and Called into Life.

Growth: Your Kingdom Come
£15.00   0 7151 4904 0
This Growth book looks in depth at two main issues, the Beatitudes and the Kingdom

Youth Emmaus
£19.95   0 7151 4988 1
Aimed specifically at young people aged 11–16, Youth Emmaus tackles the basics of the Christian faith. (Includes CD-ROM).